WORK SMARTER

500+ Online Resources
Today's Top Entrepreneurs
Use to Increase Productivity
and Achieve Their Goals

Nick Loper

Disclaimer

This book is intended for informational purposes only.

This book includes information, products, and services by third parties. These Third Party Materials consist of products and opinions expressed by their owners. As such, the author does not assume responsibility or liability for any Third Party material or opinions.

The publication of such Third Party Materials does not constitute the author's guarantee of any information, instruction, opinion, products, or services contained within the Third Party Material. The use of recommended Third Party Material does not guarantee any success and/or earnings related to you or your business. Publication of such Third Party Material is simply a recommendation and an expression of the author's own opinion of that material.

Links to Third Party Resources may be affiliate links, meaning the author may receive compensation if a service is ultimately purchased from such a link.

No part of this publication shall be reproduced, transmitted, or sold in whole or in part in any form, without the prior written consent of the author. All trademarks and registered trademarks appearing in this book are the property of their respective owners.

Users of this guide are advised to do their own due diligence when it comes to making business decisions and all information, products, and services that have been provided should be independently verified by your own qualified professionals. By reading this guide, you agree that the author is not responsible for the success or failure of your business decisions relating to any information presented in this book.

Your Free Bonus

As a small token of thanks for buying this book, I'd like to offer a free bonus gift exclusive to my readers.

This action-packed pdf is called *53 Takeaways from the World's Best Business Books* and has valuable lessons for every small business.

In this FREE bonus you'll learn:

– How to Maximize Your Return on Time.

– The Fundamental Differences Between Millionaires and the Rest of Us.

– 6 Ways to Send Your Sales Through the Roof.

– The Most Important Measure of Customer Satisfaction.

– How to Stand Out in a Crowded Marketplace.

– And much more!

You can download the free gift here:

http://www.sidehustlenation.com/FREE

Introduction

This list of resources is for entrepreneurs by entrepreneurs. I'm sure some of the tools you've already heard of and are using every day in your work, but I guarantee some will be new to you.

That's the beauty of asking *more than 800 business owners* for their top online resources; you're bound to get some great diversity in the responses.

And as entrepreneurs, we're always looking for ways to work smarter and tools to help make our lives easier.

My interest in – and appreciation for – the "tools of the trade" goes back to elementary school. My dad would refuse to help me with my homework until I sharpened my pencil.

The dull, blunt pencil didn't bother me at the time, but it was his gentle way of saying the tools you work with matter.

The resources named in this book are the sharpest pencils out there, helping small business owners get more done than ever before.

Methodology

I set out to compile the list of online resources named by today's top entrepreneurs, partially out of curiosity and partially because I knew the resulting list would be nothing short of epic.

Some of these may be obvious to you, but unknown to other people. I pride myself on being fairly savvy when it comes to this stuff, yet I still discovered dozens of awesome tools I'd never heard of before – including some of the most popular responses.

Many of the responses come from guests of the top-rated Entrepreneur on Fire podcast, where John Lee Dumas hosts some of the most accomplished and productive entrepreneurs on the planet.

The show, with nearly 1000 episodes in the bank, makes for an outstanding and high-caliber crowdsourcing opportunity.

How to Use This Guide

The resources in this guide are sorted first by category, and then alphabetically by the number of votes. That means the most popular resources and tools are the ones listed first in each section.

The names of the resources are clickable and a URL is listed for each one that got 2 or more votes.

The great news? The majority of these tools are free, offer a basic version for free, or offer a free trial. Where applicable, pricing is noted and is accurate as of press time.

Feel free to skip around; there is no right or wrong order to consume these. This book does not follow a storyline or narrative – it's simply meant to help you discover the tools you need to run a better, smarter business.

Table of Contents

Quick Start: The Top 24

If you're wondering what the most-recommended resources were in the study, look no further. Here they are in the order of votes received.

1. Google Drive / Google Docs – Web-based office software and file sharing.

2. Asana – Teamwork without email.

3. Trello – Organization and team collaboration tool.

4. Dropbox – Cloud-based file sharing and storage.

5. Basecamp – Online project management software.

6. Evernote – Powerful cross-device note-taking app.

7. LinkedIn – The professional social network.

8. Google – The world's leading search engine.

9. Boomerang – Enhance your Gmail experience.

10. Rapportive – Shows contact details and social connections in your inbox.

11. Facebook – The world's largest social network.

12. Canva – Online image editing tool.

13. Buffer – Space out your social media sharing.

14. ScheduleOnce – Scheduling application.

15. Fiverr – The marketplace for goods and services starting at $5.

16. HootSuite – Your social media control room.

17. Twitter – A steady stream of content and connections.

18. WordPress – Powerful free website building software.

19. Wunderlist – A simple to-do list and organization app.

20. Scrivener – A word processor for authors.

21. WorkFlowy – A simple organization tool.

22. PicMonkey – Online image editing tool.

23. Google Analytics – Free website traffic and audience information.

24. Google Hangouts – Free online meeting software, with recording and webinar capabilities.

Quick Start: The Category Winners

Beyond the overall top vote-getters are the standout tools in each category. These are the resources that won their "best in breed."

Accounting and Legal (tie)

Mint.com – Track all your accounts in one place.

YouNeedABudget.com – Personal budget and finance software.

Calendar Management

ScheduleOnce – Integrated online appointment scheduling tool.

Communication and Meetings

Google Hangouts – Free voice and video calls.

Content Creation

Canva – Online image editing tool.

Customer Relationship Management

Infusionsoft – Robust CRM software.

Ecommerce and Payments (tie)

Gumroad – Shopping cart software for digital products.

Shopify – Build an online store.

Education

Google – The world's leading search engine.

Email (tie)

Boomerang – Add powerful features to Gmail.

Rapportive – Shows contact details and social connections in your inbox.

Entertainment

Spotify – 20 million songs on demand.

File Sharing and Storage

Google Drive / Google Docs – Web-based office software and file sharing.

Health and Wellness

Gratitude Journal – Improve your happiness.

Marketing

Google Analytics – Free website traffic and audience information.

Networking

Meetup – Local events matching your interests.

News

Zite / Flipboard – Curated news app.

Outsourcing

Fiverr – The marketplace for goods and services starting at $5.

Productivity

Evernote – Powerful cross-device note-taking app.

Social Media

LinkedIn – The professional social network.

Team and Project Management

Asana – Teamwork without email.

Travel (tie)

Airbnb – Peer-to-peer lodging network.

TripIt – Travel organization tool.

Websites, Blogs, and Podcasts

Entrepreneur on Fire – Your daily dose of inspiration.

Accounting and Legal Resources

Between income statements, balance sheets, invoicing clients, accounts payable, tax forms, payroll, contracts, and more – the administrative burdens of running a business can be confusing, time-consuming, and expensive.

These are the top resources shared to help ease the pain of small business accounting, budgeting, and expense reports so you can focus on the core elements of your operation to make sure those net income numbers keep going up!

Mint

(2 votes!)

Mint is a free tool that does all the work of organizing and categorizing your assets and spending so you can see where every dime goes and make smarter money decisions.

I also recently started playing around with Personal Capital, which has similar functionality but is more aimed at investing and growing your nest egg.

URL: mint.com

Pricing: Free!

YouNeedaBudget.com

(2 votes!)

You Need a Budget is personal budgeting software for small businesses, individuals, and married couples. Keep track of your income, expenses, savings, debt, and cash flow to take charge of your finances.

URL: youneedabudget.com

Pricing: The software costs $60 but has a 34-day free trial.

Clerky - Legal forms and documents for startups, starting at $99.

Cozy - Property management software for landlords to screen tenants, run credit reports, and collect rent online.

Indiegogo - The world's largest global crowdfunding platform.

inDinero - Expense management software for small business owners, with taxes, accounting, and payroll services.

Kabbage - Kabbage offers fast, flexible lines of credit for small businesses. Where banks can take weeks to decide if you qualify, Kabbage delivers funds in as little as 7 minutes. Interest rates vary based on risk and credit history.

Kickstarter - Crowdfunding platform to raise funds for your next product or project.

Outright - Online bookkeeping software for small businesses for $9.99 per month. (Now owned by GoDaddy.)

Shoeboxed - Shoeboxed is the fastest way to turn a pile of receipts into digital data to save you time, money, and hassle when it's time to do your expense reports and taxes.

SignEasy - Electronic document signing, starting at $5 a year.

Xero - Online small business accounting services starting at $9 per month.

Calendar Management and Scheduling Tools

Keeping your calendar organized is a top priority, both for meeting times and for personal blocks of time to get things done. I used an annual paper day planner for years before going all digital with Google Calendar.

These are the top tools for managing your calendar and scheduling appointments so you can be available to those who need to speak with you and stay productive at the same time.

ScheduleOnce

(11 votes!)

Easy to use calendar app where you can show your available meeting times in a personalized "meet me" URL. For example, mine looks like meetme.so/nickloper.

I'm a fan and use this tool to set up almost all of my meetings! I can block out certain times and allow bookings in 15-60 minute increments when I'm available. It's a massive time-saver because it eliminates the 6-email back-and-forth of trying to find a time that works for both parties.

The service also includes features like multiple calendars and automatic email reminders in advance of your meeting.

URL: scheduleonce.com

Pricing: Plans start at $5/month and come with a 14-day free trial.

TimeTrade

(4 votes!)

TimeTrade is an online appointment scheduler that makes it easy for customers and prospects to schedule time with the right people inside a company. Consumers can book an appointment to connect with you based on the meeting times you have available.

Similar to ScheduleOnce above, this tool helps streamline the meeting process to give you more time to dedicate to your customers and get more done.

URL: timetrade.com

Pricing: A free plan is available but limited to 5 appointments per month. The Professional plan is $49 per year and comes with a 30-day free trial.

Google Calendar

(3 votes!)

I'd be lost without with my Google Calendar telling me what I've got going on each day. I can share it with others, sync it with my phone, and connect it to other calendar apps, like ScheduleOnce.

URL: google.com/calendar

Pricing: Free!

Assistant.to

(2 votes!)

Share your available meeting times and book appointments directly within your email, for free.

URL: assistant.to

Pricing: Free!

Cozi

(2 votes!)

The calendar and organization app for busy families, with free and paid versions available. Share shopping lists, to-do items, and more.

URL: cozi.com

Pricing: Free!

Sunrise Calendar

(2 votes!)

Sunrise is a free calendar made for Google Calendar, Exchange and iCloud. With an beautiful intuitive design and apps for iOS and Android, Sunrise is a new calendar experience that will make your life easier.

URL: calendar.sunrise.am

Pricing: Free!

YouCanBook.me

(2 votes!)

An online appointment booking and calendar integration service that gives you a personalized scheduling page.

URL: youcanbook.me

Pricing: Free and premium plans are available.

Appointment Core - Automate your appointment setting process with Infusionsoft and Google Calendar by letting your prospects and customers know when you're available to meet with them. Starts at $27 per month.

Boomerang Calendar - Schedule meetings with one email and highlight your available/busy time slots, all from inside Gmail.

Calendly - Calendar and appointment booking tool that integrates with Google Calendar. Free and premium versions are available.

Doodle - A simple scheduling app with both free and premium versions.

Eventbrite - Host meetups, events and conferences with Eventbrite's well-designed ticketing system. The fee is 2.5% of the ticket price, plus $1 per ticket, plus a 3% credit card processing fee.

iCalendar - $2.99 smartphone app for managing your iCal, Google, Exchange, Outlook, and Yahoo! calendars.

Communication and Meetings

It's a rare business that can succeed without any outside input or communication, which makes these communication tools all the more important.

Thankfully we have an unbelievable array of meeting resources at our fingertips that allow us to reach anyone in the world at a moment's notice. Most of the resources here are free or very affordable and rely on voice-over-IP technology.

Google Hangouts

(7 votes!)

Google Hangouts is free software for video conferencing and group meetings with up to 10 participants. I'm using Hangouts to host to my weekly mastermind sessions.

It's also great for video interviews and unlike Skype, Google still allows you to do screen sharing for free, which makes Hangouts a great tool for conducting live training with remote staff.

Hangouts are integrated with Google+ and you can use the "Hangouts on Air" feature through YouTube to host more than 10 participants and set up your own webinars.

URL: google.com/hangouts

Pricing: Free!

Skype

(6 votes!)

Skype is a popular voice-over-IP calling service that lets you make voice or video calls to anyone else in the world for free as long as they have a Skype account. You can also call phones and landlines for very affordable rates.

Skype is an essential tool for anyone doing business internationally and I find myself logged in all day long. In fact, as I'm writing this at 9:00 in the morning, I've already been on Skype with a client in Norway and team members in India and Macedonia.

I use Skype to conduct video interviews with new team members and to record all my podcast sessions. These features, along with the screen-sharing capability, make Skype a powerful communications tool.

URL: skype.com

Pricing: Skype-to-Skype calls are always free, and you can call phone numbers from 2.3 cents per minute. Their "Unlimited World" plan, which includes unlimited calls to virtually anywhere on the planet, is just $13.99 per month.

HipChat

(4 votes!)

HipChat is instant messaging built for smaller businesses. There are no ads, obscure screen names, or failed file transfers.

Users can collaborate in real-time with colleagues and clients in private chat rooms. It's hosted so you don't have to worry about managing a server or upgrading software to get the latest features.

URL: hipchat.com

Pricing: The service is free for up to 5 people. Beyond that, it's $2 per user per month with a 30-day free trial period. There are no long-term contracts.

Voxer

(4 votes!)

Voxer works like a walkie-talkie, but unlike other push-to-talk services and systems, Voxer also has integrated text, photo, and location sharing which can be sent alongside voice messaging.

You can talk to individuals or groups, selecting up to 15 chat participants to communicate with at once (or up to 500 using Voxer Pro or Voxer Business). The service use TLS/SSL for over-the-wire/air communication for security.

URL: voxer.com

Pricing: There are 3 plans: Voxer, Voxer Pro, and Voxer Business. Voxer is free application for consumer use.

Voxer Pro is $2.99 per month. It's for consumers looking for more robust features.

Voxer Business is $9.95 per month and offers a solution for companies seeking more control, access, and ownership over their business communications and data.

Google Voice

(2 votes!)

Google Voice offers a free and low cost Voice-Over-IP calling service, and you can register for your own local phone number as well.

I've been using Google Voice more lately, but I'm having routine call quality issues I don't get on Skype or on my cell phone.

The big advantage of Google Voice is in making international calls for almost nothing. I've used the service to make hotel reservations in Thailand and to arrange a venue rental in Mexico.

URL: google.com/voice

Pricing: Free calls to the US and low per-minute rates for international calls.

GoToMeeting

(2 votes!)

GoToMeeting is extremely simple software to hold unlimited online meetings. You can start a meeting and share your screen with just a click.

The collaboration is face to face with HDFaces video conferencing. Attendees can join from a Mac, PC, tablet or phone, and add their input via VoIP or telephone.

Salespeople can turn calls into instant demos and highly engaging product walkthroughs.

URL: gotomeeting.com

Pricing: There are two pricing plans - The first is $49 per month for unlimited meetings for up to 25 attendees. The second plan is $69 per month for up to 100 attendees. Both come with a 30-day free trial.

Vocaroo

(2 votes!)

Vocaroo is an online voice recorder that can be shared with others. You can use it to send a voicemail to someone's email address or just save it for your own purposes.

The service is free and you don't even have to register.

A couple things to be aware of: Vocaroo asks you not to use the service for anything too important, and doesn't guarantee how long your message will last before they delete it - it's likely to expire after a few months.

URL: vocaroo.com

Pricing: Free!

Call Ruby - Get a professional, U.S.-based virtual receptionist for your business, starting at $239 per month.

Eyejot - Eyejot is the perfect platform for creating and sending video messages to family and friends. While applications like FaceTime and Skype are ideal for live video, it's often challenging getting everyone online at the same time. Free and premium versions are available.

GoToWebinar - Easy-to-use multimedia presentation software to reach (and sell to) large audiences right from your desk. Starts at $79 per month after 30-day free trial.

HeyTell - A free smartphone app for instant voice communication.

Join.Me - Join.me is designed to be intuitive and accessible presentation and meeting software, providing features that you'll use every day for everything from show-and-tell to formal client presentations. A free basic plan is available and premium features start at $13/mo.

KiwiLive - Audience interaction software for live events.

Livestream - Livestream provides a place to broadcast live events to the web, with both free and paid options.

Olark - Add a live chat widget to your website to interact with customers and answer questions in real time. The free plan supports up to 20 chat sessions per month and premium plans start at $15/mo.

Squiggle - Squiggle is an free open-source messaging service that lets you chat with other people on your LAN network.

Stealth Seminar - Stealth Seminar provides webinar software for live, automated, or hybrid live/recorded events. The service is $70 per month with a $97 set up fee.

Ting - Ting is an affordable cell phone service with no long-term contracts. Bring your own Sprint device, keep your same phone number, and enjoy an average monthly bill of $21 a month per line. (Varies based on usage.)

Viber - Viber lets you make free calls and send text and picture messages to other Viber users for free. You only need to pay when you contact non-Viber users.

WeChat - WeChat is a free smartphone messaging service.

WorldTimeBuddy - WorldTimeBuddy is a free tool that shows time zones, converts time, and schedules meetings.

Zoom - "The Cloud Meeting Company." Zoom connects users through cloud-based sharing with fees ranging from $0 - $49.99 per month.

Content Creation Tools

Content is the currency of online business, and this section shares the top tools to help you create awesome, valuable, shareable content.

Your content, whether it's in the form of blog posts, books, guest posts, podcasts, webinars, or videos, is a primary means for new customers to discover your work. To get the creative juices flowing on what kind of content you could create, think of the questions your target customers might have and what problems they face. Answer those, and you'll have material for years.

Canva

(12 votes!)

Canva is graphic design made simple. You can create beautiful free designs for blog graphics, presentations, business cards, flyers, social media profiles, invitations, and so much more.

A great-looking graphic is vital to social media success as images tend to get shared more than any other type of content, and Canva helps you look like a Photoshop pro.

URL: canva.com

Pricing: Canva is free to use, and you can access their giant library of stock images for just $1 per image.

WordPress

(8 votes!)

WordPress is the leading website building software in the world. Don't be quick to dismiss it is merely a blogging platform because it is much more than that. In fact, WordPress powers more than 20% of the world's top 10 million sites.

Users can choose from thousands of free and premium themes and an extensive library of plugins to create a beautiful and functional website.

Because of its popularity, there is an entire ecosystem of support and developers who specialize in WordPress. That means that whatever tweaks or updates you need done, you can get it done professionally and affordably.

My sites runs WordPress and I love it! Even though I'm not a programmer, I can usually find a way to make things look and function the way I want.

URL: wordpress.org

Pricing: Free!

PicMonkey

(7 votes!)

PicMonkey is an online image editing service that lets you to add cool special effects, touch up, and design your photos.

This is the perfect quick tool to use to create shareable graphics for social media. You can add text captions or quotes over your pictures in a variety of fun fonts or use it to build your own memes.

I'm a newcomer to PicMonkey but have already started using it to make the "featured images" for my blog. It's much easier to work with than my previous image manipulation efforts, which generally involved a mix of PhotoScape, Paint, Word, and PowerPoint.

Some friends of mine even used PicMonkey to create the cover art for their podcast.

URL: picmonkey.com

Pricing: Free and paid versions available. The "Royale" version is $4.99 per month or $33 per year and includes access to premium effects, fonts, overlays, and textures.

Scrivener

(7 votes!)

Scrivener is a word processor and project management tool all in one. Designed especially for authors, its interface makes it easier to manage, edit, and rearrange content in long-form writing projects.

You can easily access your outline, research, and mind-mapping, and create your masterpiece in any order the words flow. Then, use the built-in formatting wizard to prepare your book for Amazon Kindle and other platforms.

The authors I've talked to swear by Scrivener and say, "There's no going back," to Microsoft Word after you've had a taste.

URL: literatureandlatte.com

Pricing: The software costs around $40 and comes with a 30 day free trial.

Skitch

(5 votes!)

Use Skitch to take a screenshot, add your own markup and comments, then share for free.

The application provides you with all the tools you need to visually communicate ideas, share feedback and collaborate with friends and co-workers. You can use an existing image or capture a new one, then add arrows, add shapes, or write on it with the pen or highlighter tool.

URL: evernote.com/skitch

Pricing: Free!

CreateSpace

(3 votes!)

Create a paperback version of your self-published book and sell it on Amazon. CreateSpace is print-on-demand so there's no minimum order. You are provided with all of the necessary tools and services to complete your manuscript and begin distribution.

I recommend CreateSpace for all Kindle authors, and love having a physical copy of my books to show people or use in videos to add credibility.

URL: createspace.com

Pricing: Free to set-up your account and upload your books. Physical proofs cost as little as $2.50 per copy, plus shipping.

Keynote

(3 votes!)

Keynote is the built-in presentation software for Mac. Create winning presentations and design beautiful looking slides with this free tool.

URL: apple.com/mac/keynote

Pricing: Free (with computer purchase)

Envato

(2 votes!)

Envato is the parent company for marketplaces like ThemeForest (for premium WordPress themes), GraphicRiver (for graphics), VideoHive (for video content), AudioJungle (for music), CodeCanyon (for software) and more. A great resource for the building blocks needed to create your online masterpiece.

URL: envato.com/sites

Pricing: Varies based on what you need. Graphics and audio/video clips start at $1, and premium WordPress themes generally range from $20-100.

Hemingway App

(2 votes!)

This handy online tool gives your writing a readability score and suggestions to improve it. I sometimes will run my email and blog post drafts through it to see how I could make them easier to read.

URL: hemingwayapp.com

Pricing: Free!

Ommwriter

(2 votes!)

Ommwriter is a writer's platform for creativity.

It's a "minimalist" full-screen word-processing program available for both PC and Mac. There are free and premium versions, with the paid software offering background sound and PDF export options. Both versions have background color, which is a nice change from the white background we are used to in other applications.

For some writers, a negative is that it offers only four sizes each of four different fonts. Also, Ommwriter uses a very small underscore cursor that can be difficult to spot when editing text and moving around in a document. Overall, the idea behind this minimalist software was to make the user focus and concentrate on writing itself.

URL: ommwriter.com

Pricing: Ommwriter Dana I is free and Ommwriter Dana II is the paid version, but with a twist; they only accept payment in the form of donations.

Animoto - Create and share beautiful videos. The free plan supports videos up to 30 seconds, and premium plans start at $5 per month.

AppCooker - AppCooker is a popular mobile app prototyping tool. You can test drive your app quickly and easily, without coding! Priced at $19.99.

Appendipity - Premium WordPress themes for podcasters.

Auphonic - This resource helps podcasters automatically level out their audio files and tag them for distribution. Free and premium plans are available.

Awesome Screenshot - This free browser extension helps you create screen capture images of webpages and allows you to mark them up with text, shapes, and symbols.

Balsamiq Mockups - Balsamiq is a wireframing tool for websites and user interface design. You can quickly make a few sketches of your design with plenty of UI elements to choose from. Then share with your clients, stakeholders, or allow the Balsamiq community members to provide feedback. The software is $12 a month or $79 to buy outright.

Coda - A simple text editor to write and test code for the web. Priced at $99.

CopyScape - Make sure no one is copying your content online, or find out if any of the outsourced writing you paid for is plagiarized. Free and premium versions are available.

dafont.com - A broad collection of unique and free downloadable fonts to use on your website, graphics, print materials, and more.

eCamm - Popular audio and video recording software for Mac and iOS applications.

FocusWriter - Focus Writer is a free lightweight basic text writer, designed to be free of the distractions of complex word processing applications.

GitHub - Online development project hosting, includes source-code browser, in-line editing, wikis, and ticketing. Free for public open-source code.

Haiku Deck - Haiku Deck is free software that helps you create masterpiece presentations.

Kraken.io - Compress the images on your website for faster load times with Kraken's free online tool. I use a similar service called TinyPNG.com and a free WordPress plugin called WP Smush it.

Live Writer - Windows Live Writer makes it easy to add photos and videos to your blog and format like a pro.

LogoGarden - Build your own logo in minutes for free from a massive library of starter images and fonts. Only pay when you need a high resolution copy of the logo file.

MacJournal - MacJournal is a great way to record your thoughts, special moments, daily triumphs and tribulations. You can use it to add photos and videos directly from your Dropbox account (detailed later in File Sharing and Storage). The software is $39.95.

MediaWiki - A free open source software platform to build your own wiki resource.

Medium - A free platform to share and receive feedback on your writing or just enjoy reading and rating others who contribute to Medium from around the world.

Nitro PDF - Use Nitro PDF to create high quality PDF documents that anyone can view. You can create PDFs directly from Office, or convert PDF files into Microsoft Word, Excel, and PowerPoint files. The software is $139.99 and comes with a 14-day free trial.

OurWiki - Free software to create your own wiki site or page.

Pages - Pages is a word processor for Mac that allows you to customize fonts, styles, and character and line spacing. Use it to create awesome reports, resumes, and documents. Priced at $9.99.

Pixlr - Pixlr is a free image creation tool with over 600 effects, overlays, and borders to personalize your images.

PowerPoint - Microsoft's famous presentation software is still one of my go-to tools for designing ebooks, slide decks, recording voiceover video tutorials, and more. PowerPoint comes bundled with Office or is $6.99 per month, or $69.99 to purchase separately.

PowerPoint is an underrated gem. I used it to create the presentations that landed on the homepage of SlideShare and my podcast cover art. My wife's a fan too, saying, "I can do things in PowerPoint you can't even dream of." And now you know what conversations are like at our house.

ProPrompter - ProPrompter is a high quality mobile teleprompter that works with the iPad, other tablet devices, and all smartphones. This is for the reporter, actor, television host, etc., that's constantly on the go. The software is $9.99, but an additional hardware investment may be required for best results.

Recordit.co - Free screen recording software that helps you quickly turn your recordings into animated gifs.

RecordPad - RecordPad is ideal for recording voice and other audio to add to digital presentations, creating an audio book, or for simply recording a message.

Rhymer - A free rhyming dictionary to find for rhymes for lyrics, song writing, poetry and advertisements.

Screencast-o-Matic - Free screen recordings for unlimited videos up to 15 minutes in length each, and just $15 a year for unlimited recording. This is the tool I use for all my screen recordings.

SeattleClouds.com - This tool helps non-technical people build mobile apps. Choose a template, easily edit and format your content, then add pictures and multimedia files. Pricing starts at $14.99 per month.

Sketchup - Use Sketchup's free software to sketch in 3D! It's easy to apply colors and textures that bring your sketches to life.

Slick Write - Slick Write is a free proofreading tool that checks your writing for potential stylistic mistakes and other features of interest.

SquareSpace - With just a few clicks, you can create a beautiful custom website using SquareSpace. Pricing ranges from $8 to $20 per month.

Strikingly - Strikingly helps you design and launch a beautiful mobile-ready website. It's free if you don't mind a Strikingly domain, or just $8 a month to use your own domain.

TextWrangler - TextWrangler is a free lightweight text editor.

Unsplash - Beautiful royalty-free photography.

Wideo - Create and share great-looking animated explainer videos. Free and premium versions available.

Word Swag - The $2.99 Word Swag app "automagically" turns your words into beautiful photo text designs to generate more interest and engagement on social media.

CRM Tools

CRM software, or Customer Relationship Management, helps companies track their engagement with each client they do business with.

These tools can help you organize sales leads and prospects, manage your communication and outreach efforts, and build lasting loyalty to your product or service.

Many small businesses and solopreneurs run CRM in their heads or in Excel spreadsheets, but as you grow, it can make sense to invest in a more robust system to make sure customers don't fall through the cracks.

Infusionsoft

(6 votes!)

Infusionsoft is a completely integrated software system that includes email marketing, CRM, e-commerce, sales management, contact management, sales & marketing reporting, and more.

Your dashboard is fully customizable so that you can easily see the data and key performance indicators that are most important to you. Infusionsoft is powerful, and there are many training resources and tutorial videos to help you unlock its full potential.

URL: infusionsoft.com

Pricing: Prices ranges from $199 per month (for companies with basic marketing automation needs) to $379 per month (for companies with both an online store and a sales team).

RelateIQ

(4 votes!)

RelateIQ aims to improve the way you engage with clients. You can automate messages, set reminders, and keep track of communication with algorithms in place to improve your business.

The company's software automatically logs progress on the phone, in email, and inside calendars so salespeople and their managers retain the most accurate information. The end goal is to help you close more deals and have a closer relationship with your existing customers by eliminating the pain points of other CRM systems and delivering a smarter solution.

URL: relateiq.com

Pricing: Pricing for RelateIQ starts at $49 per month, and Business plans are $99 per user/month. All plans include a 30-day free trial.

Highrise

(3 votes!)

Highrise was built by the 37signals/Basecamp team to organize your emails, conversations, notes, proposals, etc. You can receive reminders to follow up on calls, attend meetings, or reply to an email.

URL: highrisehq.com

Pricing: Priced at $24 per month.

Insightly

(2 votes!)

Insightly is powerful and affordable online customer relationship and project management software. It integrates with your email, file sharing programs, and social media networks to help you keep an eye on your sales prospects or other important people in your business.

URL: insightly.com

Pricing: Free for up to two users, with premium plans starting at $12 per user per month.

Pipedrive

(2 votes!)

Pipedrive is a CRM solution geared specifically for sales professionals. The most noticeable feature for Pipedrive is their easy drag-and-drop editing of each deal along your sales pipeline, providing instant updates for your sales team as well as clear at-a-glance organization.

Pipedrive is quick to setup and easy to learn. It runs in any web browser, making it accessible from anywhere. There is a mobile app available for iOS devices as well.

To "seed" the system initially, you can import your existing email contacts and sales leads.

URL: pipedrive.com

Pricing: Pipedrive is $9 per user/month, with a free trial available.

Zoho

(2 votes!)

Give your sales team the perfect set of apps, to help close more business deals in less time. Be right where your customers are, with apps to help your business engage with them.

URL: zoho.com

Pricing: Starts at $12 per user per month.

Hatchbuck - Hatchbuck is simple, intelligent CRM software that automates your sales and marketing efforts overnight. "Turn emails into conversations, website visitors into handshakes, and customers into raving fans." Priced from $99 per month.

Intercom - Gather intelligence and streamline your customer communication by putting it all under one messaging and tracking system. Free and premium options are available.

Less Annoying CRM - Less Annoying CRM is designed specifically for small businesses to be easier to use than other systems. Priced at $10 per user per month after a 30-day free trial.

Lifecycle Market Workshop - All you have to do is download your free Lifecycle Marketing Planner from Infusionsoft and you will gain free workshop access. You will learn how to attract new customers and how to continue to profit with the ones you already have.

Nimble - Nimble is a social CRM platform that pulls all your contacts and connections into one place so you can easily manage and communicate with them. Priced at $15 per month per user.

Ontraport - Ontraport is a full-featured CRM service for small business. Pricing starts at $297 per month for up to 25,000 contacts.

Salesforce - Salesforce is one of the most popular sales platforms around. Use it to keep track of closed and open deals, schedule meetings, and organize notes and leads. Pricing from $5 to $300 per user/month.

Satori - Satori lets you sync your calendar, collect online payments, set up questionnaires, and benefit from custom branding. This lightweight CRM system integrates with Google Calendar and MailChimp. Priced from $25 to $45 per month after 30-day free trial.

Solve360 - Solve360 is an online workplace to improve team productivity and collaboration, grow your client database, and easily manage your contacts. You can also set reminders, organize events, and track emails. Pricing starts at $39/month.

Zendesk - Customer support software that accepts ticket requests from any channel-email, web, social, phone, or chat, and offers an easy way for users to help themselves, quickly find what they need, and minimize their frustration. Pricing starts at $1 per agent per month.

Ecommerce and Payments Resources

If you're selling any kind of product or service, you need a way to collect money from customers. In fact, one of the most crucial rules of sales is to make it EASY for customers to pay you.

(I had to turn away a couple of friendly door-to-door cold callers recently because they wouldn't take cash!)

These tools will help you set up an online store and accept payments on the go.

Gumroad

(2 votes!)

Beautifully-designed shopping cart software for digital products. It's free to start, and your fee is 5% of the each transaction. Gumroad also supports Pay What You Want pricing.

URL: gumroad.com

Pricing: No set-up fees and 5% of each transaction.

Shopify

(2 votes!)

Shopify is a powerful ecommerce website solution that gives you everything you need to create an online store. They offer more than 100 quality-checked themes and more than 600 applications to automate many of your business processes.

Shopify lets you integrate a streamlined shopping cart into your site to offer products for sale and handles the payment processing as well. It integrates with WordPress and other website platforms, and is customizable to match the look and feel or your business.

URL: shopify.com

Pricing: Shopify starts at $29 per month, plus credit card transaction fees. You can try Shopify free for 14 days.

BigCommerce - Set up a shopping cart and sell products on your website. Pricing from $35 per month.

CamelCamelCamel - Set price alerts for Amazon products. Pricify.com promises to do the same for a wider number of stores.

Circle Plus - Accept credit card payments with your phone.

LevelUp - One-touch mobile payments, rich analytics, processing savings, and ROI-driven campaigns that will make your business happy.

PayPal Here - A credit card reader that works with your smartphone.

SamCart - SamCart is a shopping cart for information marketers and internet marketers selling digital products online. Pricing starts at $59 per month.

Square - Accept payments on the go with Square's credit card reader for your smartphone. The service starts at 2.75% per swipe.

Stripe - Simple and secure payment processing service that's just 2.9% per swipe plus a $0.30 transaction fee.

Educational Resources

"Anyone who stops learning is old, whether at twenty or eighty. Anyone who keeps learning stays young." –Henry Ford

Entrepreneurs never stop learning!

I like to look at each day and each project as a potential learning experience. Even if things don't go the way I expected, that's OK because I learned something new for next time.

The same is true in your interactions with other people. Bill Nye explains, "Everyone you will ever meet knows something you don't."

And Thomas Edison quipped, "We don't know a millionth of one percent about anything." I love that quote because it really drives home the fact there will always be more knowledge to soak up, more experiences to gain, and more practical wisdom to apply in our lives and in our work.

My favorite educational resource? Books and podcasts.

These are the top educational resources named.

Google

(14 votes!)

I hesitated to include this one since we use Google every day without thinking, but it did get 14 votes. (Funny, no one mentioned Bing...)

Google is a one-stop place to research, collect data, store documents, and much-much more. Google search can be used to find anything you can possibly think of, in different categories, such as blogs, news, academic articles, maps, videos, images, and more.

It's a little frightening to think of how much I rely on Google each day but there's no denying it is an essential problem-solving tool for any entrepreneur.

I constantly make "how to" searches to troubleshoot issues that come up. Just the other night, our TV had a weird narrator describing everything that was happening on the screen. I couldn't figure out how to shut her off, but Google had the answer.

URL: google.com

Pricing: Free!

Clarity.fm

(4 votes!)

Clarity connects entrepreneurs with experts and advisors in their industry for on-demand question-and-answer sessions starting at $1 per minute. You can search by expertise and set up a call with a qualified professional.

The pricing is very transparent with by-the-minute billing, which encourages people to get to the point and be respectful of everyone's time. Call quality is typically very high because after 2 negative reviews, the expert is booted from the Clarity system.

And if you have some area you're particularly knowledgeable about, there's an income opportunity here too. You can set up your expert profile, set your rate, and begin accepting calls right away.

URL: clarity.fm

Pricing: The majority of experts are available at rates between $1 and $2 per minute, but you can spend as much as $167 per minute to talk to Mark Cuban (no takers yet!).

Clarity also has an option called Clarity Live. For a $97 per month fee (advertised as an introductory price), you can attend up to 6 live video Q&A sessions and get half off regular one-on-one Clarity calls.

Pocket

(4 votes!)

The free Pocket browser extension lets you save blog posts and news articles for later viewing. It's perfect for those epic long-form articles that you just don't have time for at the moment you find them.

URL: getpocket.com

Pricing: Free!

TED

(4 votes!)

TED is a free platform dedicated to "ideas worth spreading" in science, education, social issues, the arts, and more. On their site, you can view an impressive catalog of TED Talk videos.

I had the opportunity to volunteer at a local TEDx event last year, which was pretty cool, and I like to watch TED videos on my iPad while I'm folding laundry.

URL: [ted.com](ted.com)

Pricing: Free!

Audible

(3 votes!)

Sometimes, you just don't have time to sit down and read a book. That's where Audible comes in. Audible offers audiobooks in mp3 format.

With more than 150,000 titles to choose from, including many bestsellers, you can listen to a new book each month in your car, at the gym, or while you're out walking the dog.

URL: audible.com

Pricing: An Audible subscription costs $15 per month and includes one book download. However, the first book is free with a 30-day trial.

Feedly

(3 votes!)

Feedly is a free blog reader. After Google shut down Google Reader, this is what I've been using to keep up with my favorite blogs.

Fastlane Forums

(2 votes!)

Popular online forums discussing startups and entrepreneurship around the ideas found in *The Millionaire Fastlane* by MJ DeMarco.

URL: thefastlaneforum.com

Pricing: Free!

Stitcher

(3 votes!)

Stitcher is your home for top on-demand radio and podcast content. Stream the latest in news, sports, talk, and entertainment radio anywhere in the world, or use the free Stitcher app to download episodes to your smartphone.

And of course, don't forget to subscribe to The Side Hustle Show and Entrepreneur on Fire!

URL: stitcher.com

Pricing: Free!

Lynda.com

(2 votes!)

Lynda gives you access to thousands of instructional videos with easy-to-follow tutorials on software, creative, and business skills.

URL: lynda.com

Pricing: Lynda is $25 per month (get a 7-day Free Trial!).

Skillshare

(2 votes!)

Skillshare is an online education platform where you can learn and master real-world skills taught by industry experts.

URL: skillshare.com

Pricing: $9.95 per month. (Get a free 7-day trial!)

Summary.com

(2 votes!)

Summary.com offers book summaries, webinars, videos, and more to help grow your business. You can also access your online library via iOS or Android devices.

URL: summary.com

Pricing: Priced from $9.95 to $229.

Remember, as your free bonus for buying this book you have access to my own summary guide, *53 Takeaways from the World's Best Business Books*.

Free access here:

http://www.sidehustlenation.com/free

Academic Earth - Academic Earth provides open access to free online courses from top universities.

Audiobooks.com - Another option for finding the perfect audiobook to listen to, Audiobooks.com is great for those who prefer audiobooks, or those that don't have the time to sit down and read. Like Audible, the service is also $15 per month, with the first book being free.

BizSum.com - Starting at $9.95 per summary or $225 per year, BizSum.com offers business book summaries. These can increase the productivity and efficiency of your employees, while teaching necessary skills, or can help you become a better manager and keep up with the latest ideas.

Blinkist - Blinkist gives you 15-minute summaries of the best nonfiction books. Subscriptions start at $7.99 per month.

Breakthrough DNA - An article that will tell you 8 Profit Activators You Can Trigger in Your Business Right Now.

CNET - Expert product reviews and comparisons, plus tons of free software downloads.

Duolingo - Duolingo offers free language learning software.

The Foundation - Learn the mindset and skills required to build a software business from scratch, with no programming required.

Google Prior Art - Use the prior art search to scans text for key phrases, combines them into a set of search queries, and displays the results from Google Patents, Google Scholar, Google Books, and the rest of the web.

Harvard Business Review - Ideas, articles, and advice for leaders.

iTunes - A massive library of free podcast content at your fingertips.

JSTOR - JSTOR is a free digital library of more than 2,000 academic journals, 20,000 books, and two million primary sources.

Language Immersion for Chrome - This free browser plugin translates portions of websites on the fly (and according to your settings) to help you practice a new language.

Mindsnacks - Free games for learning techniques to teach vocabulary, context, and grammar.

MIT Opensource - MIT published all of their course materials online and made them available to everyone for free.

Operation Money Suck - This short essay from John Carlton serves as a reminder to avoid all the time and money-sucking distractions that keep you from earning money, making sales, and delivering results for your clients.

Paul Graham's Essays - Venture capitalist and founder of Y-Combinator Paul Graham has published dozens of essays on technology, startups, and making a dent in the universe.

ReadItFor.Me - ReadItFor.Me are free hour-long workshops based on 12-minute animated summaries of the world's best leadership, sales, marketing and personal development books.

Reference USA - The premier source of free business and residential information for reference and research.

Scribd - Scribd is your personal digital library, where you have unlimited access to the world's largest collection of e-books and written works. Pricing starts at $8.99 per month.

Self-Help Classics - A $0.99 app that puts 39 self-help classics right on your iOS or Android device.

SparkNotes - Study guides for the world's most popular literature and other academic subjects.

StackOverflow - A free question and answer site for professional and enthusiast programmers.

Study Leadership - The Study Leadership service provides you with summaries of some the best leadership books available for reference, inspiration, and continued growth. For the cost of just a few books ($6.95 per month), you get 30 summaries a year.

The Old Reader - A social RSS reader that's free for up to 100 feeds (or $3 per month beyond that). Not only can you stream your favorite RSS feeds, you can comment and share your thoughts with others as well. It's easy to import your subscriptions from another reader and the service can be used on your computer or through their mobile app.

The Star Principle - This book by Richard Koch is $8 on Kindle and aims to share with you the secrets of high-growth high-value startups.

The Way to Wealth - The full text of this 1758 Benjamin Franklin essay is available online and still holds true today.

theSkimm - Don't have time to read through all of today's news articles? TheSkimm condenses them for you for free, highlighting all the important details.

UltraLingua - UltraLingua's software helps people language-learning or translation needs. Free and premium versions are available.

Website Magazine - Get a free subscription to this print magazine that covers online marketing, apps, analytics, research, ecommerce, social media, and more.

Wikipedia - The free online encyclopedia.

Email Tools

We tend to take email for granted, but it is a powerful communication tool even without any of these additional resources. In fact, email itself got 2 votes (including one from Seth Godin).

Email consumes so much of our daily work life; it's hard to imagine a world without it. These resources will help you be a better emailer, reclaim control of your inbox, and ultimately be more productive.

Boomerang

(12 votes!)

Boomerang is an add-on service for Gmail that lets you schedule emails to be sent at specific times, track responses, and configure automatic reminders if you don't get a reply.

Boomerang will also tell you if an email was opened and if any links were clicked.

URL: boomeranggmail.com

Pricing: Boomerang has a free Basic Plan, a $4.99 per month Personal plan, and a $14.99 per month Professional plan with advanced functionality and features. The Professional plan includes a 30-day free trial.

Rapportive

(12 votes!)

Rapportive is a free tool that shows you everything about your contacts right inside your Gmail inbox, including a profile picture, LinkedIn data, and social media accounts.

I love Rapportive and use it every day. One way it's useful is to make sure you're connecting with your email contacts on social channels as well. (I've grown my LinkedIn network considerably thanks to Rapportive.)

And another way Rapportive comes in handy is when you're trying to guess someone's email address. If you open a compose window and begin entering in common email address formats (like firstname@companyname.com), you'll know you've hit a winner when Rapportive shows a match!

URL: rapportive.com

Pricing: Free!

Contactually

(5 votes!)

Contactually is a management system with automated follow-up reminders. The service scans your contact list and you can assign people to different "buckets" such as "sales leads," "family," "friends," "co-workers," and more.

I did their free 30-day trial and was actually pretty impressed with their system of "buckets" and their suggestion algorithm on who to follow-up with is surprisingly good. Each day you'll get 4 suggestions on people you've emailed in the past but haven't been in contact with in a while.

It can be a reminder to rekindle friendships or follow up with an idle sales lead. And even if nothing immediately comes of it, it keeps you top-of-mind in case a question or need ever arises.

URL: contactually.com

Pricing: There is a free version but I've found it's pretty weak – you only get 1 suggested follow-up per day, which means the probability of it being someone you should reach out to is not great. Pricing for the premium service starts at $20 per month.

Followup.cc

(5 votes!)

Followup.cc is a useful email reminder service to help you manage your inbox and not lose track of important conversations. How it works is you bcc a followup.cc email address, like 2weeks@followup.cc and you get an automatic reminder in your inbox if you haven't heard back from the email recipient.

You can also use this just as a reminder to yourself while you're processing your email. For instance, you may not have time to deal with a certain message at the moment or it may not be urgent, but you want to get it off your plate and out of your mind. In that case, you can just forward it to 2days@followup.cc and it will be gone from your inbox for 48 hours.

I've been testing this along with a service called Nudgemail, which has similar functionality and is in free beta.

URL: followup.cc

Pricing: A free plan allows for one email account and up to 10 reminders per month, while the paid plans lift these restrictions and come with additional features for $4 to $18 per month (paid annually).

Google Apps

(4 votes!)

Google Apps for Business is a cloud-based service for individuals or any size business. It is rich with many productive and functional applications, including Gmail, Calendar, Drive, Docs, and more.

The service is perfect for small business owners who want to keep their business email in the familiar Gmail platform, but keep it totally separate from their personal account.

URL: google.com/enterprise/apps/business/

Pricing: The service has two pricing tiers: for Business, from $5 per user per month, and for Business with Vault, from $10 per user per month.

SaneBox

(4 votes!)

SaneBox analyzes your past behavior – which emails you open, which ones you reply to, and how often, and automatically sends the emails it determines to be unimportant to a separate folder. It does this without reading the content of your messages, only the senders and the subject lines.

SaneBox also allows you to "snooze" non-urgent emails, unsubscribe from unwanted newsletters with 1 click, get reminders when people don't reply to you, and move attachments to Dropbox. According to SaneBox, the tool saves an average employee over 100 hours per year.

URL: sanebox.com

Pricing: After the free 2 week trial period, you can choose from the 3 available plans starting at $7 per month.

Streak

(3 votes!)

Streak is a free tool that helps users keep track of deals and CRM from their Gmail inbox. You can know who read the email, when and where.

Streak also supports additional features like delayed sending (as Boomerang), canned responses, and auto-message organization.

URL: streak.com

Pricing: Free!

Yesware

(3 votes!)

Yesware helps salespeople track and analyze their email and deal-flow, with template and mail merge support along with follow-up reminders.

You'll know who opened your email and who clicked on your links.

URL: yesware.com

Pricing: $10 - $80 per user per month.

Chimpadeedoo

(2 votes!)

A free opt-in app from MailChimp that works even when offline. Input emails from your phone or tablet and they will sync with your MailChimp list once you get back online.

URL: mailchimp.com/chimpadeedoo

Pricing: Free! (Requires a MailChimp account.)

FollowUpThen

(2 votes!)

The FollowUpThen email reminder service is similar to Followup.cc not only in the name, but in functionality.

As points of differentiation, FollowUpThen allows for up to 50 reminders per month on their free plan, and claims to support more natural language when scheduling reminders. You can also schedule automatic reminders for as many as 15 people at once.

URL: followupthen.com

Pricing: The service is free for up to 50 reminders a month, and then only $2 per month for up to 250 reminders. Professional and Company plans are also available with additional features and functionality.

Gmail

(2 votes!)

Gmail is the world's most popular free webmail service, with 15 GB of free storage. I rely on Gmail daily and funnel all my email through my central Gmail account. It's "command central" for running an online business, and even though I know I'm not supposed to check email first thing in the morning, it's usually the first browser tab I open.

URL: gmail.com

Pricing: Free!

Inbox Pause

(2 votes!)

Allows you to "pause" your incoming email to focus on your most important tasks and projects. Just "unpause" later to see all the messages that came in.

URL: inboxpause.com

Pricing: Free!

MailChimp

(2 votes!)

MailChimp is an easy way to create and send e-mail marketing campaigns. The best part? It's beautifully designed and free for up to 2000 subscribers.

MailChimp helps you collect email addresses and manage your email list in an elegant and intuitive interface. They help you steer clear of spam complaints and make sure your messages get delivered.

URL: mailchimp.com

Pricing: Free for up to 2000 subscribers and 12000 messages per month. Beyond that, pricing starts at $30 per month and increases as your subscriber-base grows.

Unroll.me

(2 votes!)

Unroll.me is a free tool that scans your inbox and pulls in all your email newsletter subscriptions. The service allows you to bulk-unsubscribe and "roll up" the rest into a daily summary email.

URL: unroll.me

Pricing: Free!

ActiveInbox - Turns Gmail into a task manager. $40 a year.

AwayFind - AwayFind lets you step away from your inbox to avoid the constant distractions, but still get notified of urgent time-sensitive messages. Pricing starts at $5 a month.

AWeber - AWeber is a popular email marketing and list-management service starting at $19 per month. Your first month is just $1.

BatchedInbox - A free tool that lets email hit your inbox only at specified intervals to reduce distractions.

CoBook - A free unified address book for Mac.

Covideo - A video email service. $49 per month.

Gmail Labs - What's your favorite Gmail labs feature? Mine has got to be the Undo send feature!

Gmail Shortcuts - Gmail has a ton of useful keyboard commands built-in. If you take the time to learn a few of these keyboard shortcuts, you'll fly through your email faster since you never have to reach for the mouse.

Mailbox - This free app is a popular replacement for the native email apps in iOS and Android.

MailerLite - MailerLite is an email marketing service to help you send out your email newsletters. Pricing ranges from $99 - $495 per month.

TheMagicEmail.com - A free email script that works like magic to re-engage prospects and close more deals.

Entertainment Resources

All work and no play ... just doesn't work! Even entrepreneurs need some time to relax and recharge every now and then.

Spotify

(4 votes!)

Spotify is a free music player with access to more than 20 million songs. You can share and view playlists with friends for free.

URL: spotify.com

Pricing: Spotify has a free version and a paid plan for $9.99 per month, which removes the advertising and playback restrictions.

IMDB

(3 votes!)

IMDB is a free database of movies and actors. It also has movie reviews, TV shows, and lists by categories or popularity.

URL: imdb.com

Pricing: Free!

1 Second Everyday - This free app helps you capture a 1 second video every day to compile a personal video history.

Netflix - Netflix is an online streaming service for TV shows and movies. These can be watched anywhere and anytime, as long as the viewer has an internet connection and a subscription to Netflix. Subscriptions start at $8 per month, and new users can get a free 30-day trial period.

Pandora - Pandora offers free online music streaming and creates smart playlists on the fly based on the kind of music you like.

Passbook - Passbook is a native iOS app that acts as a single repository for all the movie and sports tickets, loyalty and payment cards, boarding passes, coupons, and other passes generated by all the compatible apps on your iPhone or iPod Touch.

PollStar - Pollstar is a concert venue database and the who's who of concert venue information.

Rap Genius - Rap Genius is your guide to the meaning of rap, R&B, and soul lyrics. Search by artist, song, or lyrics.

UE Boom - UE BOOM is the 360° speaker that drops bold, immersive sound in every direction. Priced at $199.99.

uTorrent - Download tons of free content from BitTorrent Bundles with automatic bandwidth management. Free and premium versions are available.

File Sharing and Storage

If you're doing any kind of business online, having some method to share and transfer files is absolutely crucial. These resources can help you securely use the cloud to back-up your important work or seamlessly collaborate with other members of your team.

In extreme cases, I've heard of some entrepreneurs storing nothing on their laptop; their entire business is in the cloud. That kind of set-up would be difficult if you're ever in a situation without Internet access, but illustrates the freedom and flexibility some of these services can provide.

Google Drive / Google Docs

(32 votes!)

Google offers a cloud storage service, known as Google Drive. Files can be stored in the cloud and shared with others for collaboration for free. In combination with their free Docs software, this was the #1 most-named resource in the study.

I use Google Docs every day, and actually used it extensively to compile this post. (I'm typing this in the Google Docs word processor right now.) It doesn't have all the functionality you get in the Microsoft Office suite, but for most tasks, it gets the job done.

There are some fun things you can do with Google Docs and your Drive account. For instance, I've used Docs to create custom surveys and embed those survey forms in websites and emails. The responses are all stored automatically in a Docs spreadsheet.

My VA and I use Google Drive to share files for editing and collaboration. Rather than each working independently on separate files on our local machines, we can work on the same file simultaneously, and even chat with each other from inside the Google Docs interface.

I was a slow adopter to move from Office into the cloud, but I like the flexibility of having the files accessible from any of my devices and even on any other computer after I log in.

URL: drive.google.com

Pricing: Google Drive is free for up to 15 GB of storage (which includes your linked Gmail account). Up to 100 GB is available for just $1.99 per month.

Dropbox

(20 votes!)

Dropbox is an excellent tool for storing files in the cloud and sharing information. It acts as an online backup and can be used to share files and sync data with others.

I use Dropbox in several ways. First, I have the WordPress Backup to Dropbox plugin that automatically backs up my site to my Dropbox account each week.

Anytime I download a new pdf ebook or white paper guide, I move the file to my Dropbox so I can read it later. Then, when I have reading time, I'll pull it up from my iPad.

And finally I use it to share files and folders with others just by sending a link. It's faster and easier than sending big attachments through email, and won't clog up your email storage limits.

URL: dropbox.com

Pricing: New accounts get 2 GB free, and you can earn more storage by referring friends. A Pro account with 100 GB is $9.99 per month.

I also use a rival service called Copy that gives new accounts 15 GB of free storage.

Wistia

(2 votes!)

Wistia is a beautifully designed video player and hosting solution. Free and premium versions are available.

URL: wistia.com

Pricing: A free account lets you host up to 50 videos, and premium plans start at $25 a month.

AudioAcrobat - AudioAcrobat records, uploads, and downloads audio and video. The service is both a recording and a hosting provider, with subscriptions starting at $20 per month.

Bluehost - Affordable web hosting starting around $5 a month.

Carbonite - Carbonite is a cloud backup service. It also provides file sharing and data syncing, all for $60 per year.

Collabshot - Collabshot is a free screen capture and annotation tool. Screenshots can be captured and shared with others for free. I've been using a free Chrome extension called AwesomeScreenshot as an alternative service.

CloudUp - Online file sharing, streaming, and storage for up to 1000 items or 200 GB free.

DocuSign - Sometimes, documents need to be signed, but that can be difficult over the internet. With DocuSign, documents can be shared and electronically signed, with subscriptions for only $10 per month.

DraftIn - DraftIn is a version control and collaboration tool for writers. There is even the option to ask a professional, such as with copy-editing or proofreading questions. Both free and paid versions are available.

Drafts App - Drafts is an Apple application that aids in note-taking, idea capture, and sharing. It is $3.99 in iTunes.

Ghostery - This free browser extension is the web's most popular privacy tool.

Kaltura - Kaltura provides the world's first and only open source online video platform. Pricing starts at $750 a month.

Microsoft BizSpark - BizSpark provides 3 years of free software, hosting, support, and visibility for startups.

PhotoStream - PhotoStream facilitates free iCloud photo and video sharing. All of your devices can view an image or video simultaneously, and you can share your stream and invite friends and family to add their own photos and video clips. Everyone can comment and access their shared streams from any iPhone, iPad, iPod touch, Mac, or PC at any time.

Screencast.com - Record screen-capture videos of your desktop, store them in the cloud, and share them with other members of your team. Get 2 GB of storage and 2 GB of bandwidth per month for free.

VIPorbit - VIPorbit keeps your desktop and devices in sync while providing online backups to protect your most valuable digital assets. Free and premium offerings are available.

Hardware

A variety of "offline" tools and resources were named, ranging from very high-tech devices to some decidedly low-tech options as well. Sometimes the latest software and apps distract us more than they help us.

Pen and Paper

(2 votes!)

Yes, good old-fashioned pen and paper got a couple votes. And truth be told, this is still my preferred to-do list "system." There's just something inherently satisfying about physically crossing something off that list!

iPad - The popular tablet device for email, social media, apps, music, reading, and more. I do most of my reading on my iPad.

Kindle - An entire library of books in the palm of your hand and without killing any trees.

Your Phone - Yes, that miracle device that never leaves your side can occasionally be used to make calls too!

Samsung Galaxy Note / Smartphone - Today's smartphone holds more computing power than Apollo 11, and gives you access to many of the other tools and resources mentioned here.

I [heart] my iPhone, and cut my monthly bill in half with Ting.

Sticky Pads - Post-it notes are the original Evernote, right? I still use them every day to take notes, do math, and make grocery lists.

Whiteboard - Keep track of projects, goals, and aspirations on your giant office whiteboard. Great for brainstorming too.

Health and Wellness Resources

Hey, if you don't have your health and happiness, all the entrepreneurial success in the world is for nothing, right?

I recently read a quote that stuck with me: *"If you don't take care of your body, where will you live?"*

These are the resources that will help you track your fitness and weight loss goals, keep you motivated, plan your meals, and even improve your sleep.

Gratitude Journal / Happy Tapper

(3 votes!)

This is the # 1 Gratitude Journal application, and it's just $0.99 in iTunes. Science says those who take a minute each day to write down what they're thankful for are happier than those who don't!

URL: happytapper.com

Pricing: $0.99 in the App Store.

Headspace

(3 votes!)

Headspace is meditation made simple. Learn online, when you want, wherever you are, in just 10 minutes a day.

URL: headspace.com

Pricing: Starts at $5 a month.

F.lux

(2 votes!)

Free software that adjust the blue light emitted by your computer monitor late at night to help you sleep better.

MyFitnessPal

(2 votes!)

A popular free calorie counter application.

5 Minute Journal - Start your day by writing down three things you are grateful for and change your day for the better. The app costs $4.99.

Ben Greenfield Fitness - Top-rated health and fitness blog and podcast.

Calm - Calm.com plays calming music and visuals for free.

DreamItAlive.com - Use this free tool to create your own online "Dreamboard" to help you visualize what you really truly want and be guided to your best possible life.

Endomondo - Track your run or other sporting pursuits. There are both free and paid versions.

Examine.com - Independent scientific information on supplements & nutrition, backed with citations to published scientific studies.

ExRx.com - A free resource for the exercise professional, coach, or fitness enthusiast featuring a comprehensive library of more than 1600 exercises, fitness assessment calculators, and reference articles.

Foodista - Recipes and cooking tips.

Guided Meditation with Sam Harris - Let bestselling author Sam Harris guide you through a brief mindfulness exercise.

My Mad Methods - Fitness and strength training blog and magazine.

Notes from the Universe - Free daily inspirational emails.

OhLife - Free daily reminder service to write about your life.

Pact - The free Pact app makes you put your money where your mouth is. You can earn money by following through on your goals of going to the gym or eating healthy, paid for by those who don't.

RSIGuard - Remedy Interactive's RSIGuard is an award-winning desktop ergonomic software solution that reduces repetitive strain injuries. Priced at$65.

Simplify Supper - Simplify Supper is a free meal planning system.

SleepCycle - A bio-alarm clock that analyzes your sleep patterns and wakes you when you are in the lightest sleep phase. $0.99.

Striiv - The $99 Striiv smartwatch will track your activity throughout the day and your sleep at night.

Marketing Resources

Use these resources to have new customers lining up out the door. Today's marketing is about measuring results and maximizing your return on investment, and these tools help you do just that.

You'll be able to track campaigns, analyze your efforts, and capture more leads and sales.

After all, the best business idea in the world will still fail if no one knows about it.

Google Analytics

(7 votes!)

Small businesses can utilize Google Analytics to track visitors to their site, conversion goals and rates, time-on-site metrics, entry paths and much more. To top it off, this is a free tool for users and has become the gold standard in website analytics software.

It installs easily with one line of code and you can begin tracking your website's performance today.

The challenge I run into with Analytics is yes, it's fun to look at, but it can be hard to figure out what ACTION to take based on the data.

A couple things to pay attention to in your Analytics account if you're not already is the percentage of your traffic that's coming from mobile devices, and the search queries your visitors are using on your site.

To view the mobile traffic data, go to Audience > Mobile > Overview. I'm always surprised to see the mobile numbers continue to climb and compare the other performance metrics to the desktop and tablet traffic. It's a good reminder to double-check how your site renders and functions on a smartphone-sized screen.

And to see the search query data (the keywords people are typing into *your* search bar, not the ones they used to find your site in Google), go to Behavior > Site Search > Overview. This will give you an honest insight into what your visitors are really looking for and can be a great way to generate new content ideas to make sure you're delivering what your visitors want.

URL: google.com/analytics

Pricing: Free!

LeadPages

(5 votes!)

LeadPages is a landing page and email opt-in form generator that integrates with all the major email service providers. It's the easiest way to build conversion optimized & mobile responsive landing pages and allows for simple split-testing to see which elements convert best.

Building an email list of prospective customers is one of the most important activities you can do to constantly be funneling leads into your business, and LeadPages is the market leader in helping you get it done.

URL: leadpages.net

Pricing: $37 per month.

Moz

(5 votes!)

Moz.com (formerly SEOmoz) helps you create, manage, and improve your online business presence. With the Moz Pro plan, the service performs in-depth research on your site and your competitors, and offers educational resources for SEO and inbound marketing.

I'm far from being an SEO-pro, but I like to check out their OpenSiteExplorer.com tool see the backlink profile and domain authority of certain sites. And if you want to know how to rank your site higher in the search engines, the Moz blog is a must-read.

URL: moz.com

Pricing: Moz Local is $49 per year and Moz Pro starts at $99 per month with a 30-day free trial.

Optimizely

(3 votes!)

Optimizely acts as your on-demand technical team for split-testing, with technology that turns your creative changes into instantly generated and deployed code.

URL: optimizely.com

Pricing: Currently they have a 30 day free trial, and paid plans start at $17/month.

OptimizePress

(3 votes!)

OptimizePress allows you to easily create beautiful and high-converting landing pages, sales pages, and membership portals, right on top of your familiar WordPress platform.

URL: optimizepress.com

Pricing: Priced starting at $97.

22Social

(2 votes!)

A full-featured Facebook marketing application to build engagement, capture leads, and drive sales all from within Facebook. This tool promises to decrease your cost to acquire a new customer and one respondent described it as "LeadPages for Facebook."

URL: 22social.com

Pricing: Free and premium versions are available.

CoSchedule

(2 votes!)

CoSchedule is a drag-and-drop WordPress editorial calendar with built-in social media sharing capabilities. Priced at $10 per month.

Heyo

(2 votes!)

Heyo is Facebook marketing for small businesses. They make it easy to create Facebook campaigns, with no coding knowledge required. You can just drag and drop the desired options, such as Google maps, email links, or other widgets, to create a mobile-optimized Facebook campaign.

URL: heyo.com

Pricing: Plans start at $25 per month.

Instant Teleseminar

(2 votes!)

Instant Teleseminar is a resource to help businesses host teleseminars and webinars, with prices ranging from $47 - $197 per month.

KISSmetrics

(2 votes!)

KISSmetrics aims to provide what Google Analytics lacks – information about *who* is accessing your website. Also be sure to check out their award-winning blog for in-depth marketing tutorials and case-studies.

URL: kissmetrics.com

Pricing: $150 - $500 per month.

Visual Website Optimizer

(2 votes!)

Use Visual Website Optimizer to increase website sales and conversions with their easy to use split-testing and visitor heat-mapping tools. You don't have to be a programmer to take advantage of this helpful service.

URL: visualwebsiteoptimizer.com

Pricing: It's free to test up to 1000 visitors in 30 days, and premium plans start at $49 per month.

AdRoll - AdRoll retargets and attempts to re-capture your website visitors by displaying advertising on sites such as Facebook and Twitter.

Alexa - Alexa is a free resource that provides information on website statistics and traffic information. You can find out how your site stacks up in terms of traffic compared to the competition.

AuctionZip - A database of live and online auctions, perfect for resellers to source inventory.

BrandVerity - Monitor your brand name online and make sure your affiliate partners are playing by the rules.

BrightTALK - Whether you need to create a webinar or join one, BrightTALK can help. Their webinar software and hosting plans help marketers grow their audiences and start at $250 per month.

Compete.com - Gather competitive intelligence on other websites in your niche, including relative traffic estimates, keyword popularity, and more. Another free tool I like is SimilarWeb.com.

Crushpath - Crushpath helps small businesses with their prospecting by helping them create compelling content and driving qualified visitors to see it. Pricing starts at $29 per month.

Google AdWords - When customers search for something on Google, relevant ads are usually displayed in the search results. Businesses can advertise using Google AdWords to make sure that their ads are being seen by relevant customers.

Google Alerts - Google Alerts is a free service that sends you an email when new articles pop up about your chosen topic.

You can use this to join in conversations that are already happening, stay on top of your niche, or monitor your reputation online. For instance, I have alerts for "side hustle," "nick loper," and "side hustle nation."

Google Insights - Google Insights provides products and advertising platforms to help users reach marketing goals. They offer analytics, marketing strategies, and planning tools at no charge.

HelloBar - Adds a free call-to-action stripe at the top of your website.

HelpAReporter.com - This free 3x daily newsletter helps connect journalists and sources. Entrepreneurs and experts can use it to get press and free publicity. If HelpAReporter (HARO) gets too crowded, try MuckRack and SourceBottle as a couple alternatives.

Hubspot Analytics - As an alternative to Google Analytics, Hubspot Analytics provides an in depth view of marketing data. It can help improve and optimize marketing efforts to get the best effect for the user. Subscriptions start at $200 per month.

InfoBlog - InfoBlog is a huge database where articles can be submitted or accessed for free.

JVZoo - Create your own affiliate program and recruit others to help sell your products or services.

Kajabi - Kajabi is an easy-to-use platform that lets you quickly create beautiful membership sites, right in your web browser. Pricing starts at $99 per month.

Lucky Orange - Use heatmaps, polls, and live chat to determine what improvements to make on your website. Priced from $10 per month with a 7-day free trial.

Marketing Land - Popular online marketing blog covering social media, email, content, mobile, search, and more.

MarketingProfs.com - Marketing resources and strategies. Join free for access to their discussion forums, seminars, and virtual conferences.

Meddle.it - Meddle is a content marketing tool for individuals and companies. Curate content that will resonate with your tribe and share it across your social platforms. Registration is free.

Moo.com - Moo wants you to get rid of your ugly VistaPrint business cards and try theirs instead.

Panjiva - Panjiva is a resource for buyers and sellers to find information about suppliers, buyers, and sales. Pricing ranges from $99 - $399/month.

PostcardMania - Your one-stop partner for direct mail lists, production, and mailing.

Postling - Postling helps small businesses maximize their social media exposure. Pricing is $10 a month for up to 5 users.

Purlem - Create personalized landing pages to boost response rates for online or offline marketing and see exactly which prospects are engaging.

QuickSprout.com - A free website evaluation tool and popular online marketing and SEO blog by Neil Patel.

Qzzr.co - Create engaging and shareable quizzes for your website or blog. There are both free and premium versions.

RadioGuestList - Like HelpAReporter above, but for radio and podcast exposure.

SearchEngineLand - SearchEngineLand is a blog about SEO and the latest news in search marketing.

SEMrush - Software for SEO and marketing professionals to research keywords, ranking, and competition. Priced from $69.95 per month.

Sensor Tower - Sensor Tower helps you take control of your visibility in the App Store and gain valuable App Intelligence insights. The service is free.

SERPWoo - SERPWoo gives you a clear picture of what's really going on in the top search engine results for a niche. Priced at $19.99 per month.

SimilarWeb - Get insightful competitive intelligence on others companies and websites in your industry for free.

Skimlinks - This free service automatically affiliates your outbound links to help monetize your traffic.

Social Lead Freak - This premium software helps you identify, target, and close highly qualified leads on social media. Priced from $97.

SumoMe - This free software helps you add well-designed popups to capture email addresses from visitors on your website.

Thrive Content Builder - I believe this is LeadPages' most viable competition at the moment. They make it easy to build customized landing pages and Thrive Leads helps turn more of your visitors into subscribers. The best part may be that the software is available as a one-time purchase (starting at $59) instead of requiring an ongoing subscription.

Triberr - Triberr is a free platform to connect with other influencers in your niche and share each other's content.

Unbounce - Unbounce helps you build and publish A/B test landing pages to improve conversions. The service is priced from $49/month to $199/month.

vCita - vCita is an all-in-one lead generation, contact management, online scheduling, and invoicing tool for small businesses. Free and premium versions are available.

Wishlist Member - Turn any WordPress site into a fully-featured membership site. Priced at $97 for one domain.

WP Bounce - Better monetize your website traffic with a call-to-action lightbox popover as visitors are about to leave. Priced at $27 as a one-time purchase.

Networking Resources

When I ask entrepreneurs for their #1 piece of advice, an answer I hear over and over again is, "Build your network." And networking doesn't have to be a dirty word. Done right, it's about the mutual exchange of value and introducing people to others who might be able to help them.

I'm dreadfully shy at networking events, but agree that connecting with new people is one of my most important daily activities. Think of it this way, if you make a good impression, you're not just meeting one person; you're meeting that person's entire network.

This works online too. Just today I read an AMAZING post about book marketing and have gone out of my way to share it with as many people as possible. By reaching one person (me), the author reached dozens more. And I'm sure many of them went on to share it as well.

These are the resources that can help build your network and make you a better networker.

Meetup

(2 votes!)

Meetup is a free service that can be used to organize meetings with others who may share common interests or goals.

URL: meetup.com

Pricing: Meetups are generally free or very cheap to attend. If you want to host a group, it's $5 per month.

The C12 Group - America's leading Christian CEO forum, with a mission to build "great businesses for a greater purpose." It's not cheap though; membership costs $1000 per month after a $1250 registration fee.

CamCard - Take a picture of business cards, and all the contact information is quickly and accurately read and saved to your smartphone.

Own It - A specialized professional network dedicated to helping small business owners and the self-employed grow thriving businesses through the power of peers. Make better, more informed decisions by tapping into the experiences of experts and people like you.

Publishers Marketplace - Publishers Marketplace for publishing professionals is used to find critical information and unique databases. It is also used for professionals to find each other and do business better electronically. The subscription fee is $25 per month.

Refresh.io - Refresh is a free app that helps prepare you for upcoming meetings and conversations by finding relevant insights about the people you're going to meet. This helps you build rapport quickly and look like you have the memory of an elephant!

SHRM - The Society for Human Resource Management is a professional organization for HR professionals.

Socialcast - Socialcast is social networking and collaboration for enterprises. This service ranges in price from $1 to $2.50 per month per user.

Spiceworks - Spiceworks is a free networking site for IT professionals and those seeking IT professionals.

Unation - Connecting the world through meaningful and relevant events, Unation helps bring businesses and citizens together.

ZabaSearch - Giant aggregated database to search for people and their information. Free and premium versions are available.

News Resources

I tend to limit my intake of general "mainstream" news, and instead prefer to find industry specific blogs and social media channels to stay informed on. The resources listed here are a healthy combination of both options – you can get your dose of world events along with a custom-curated list of stories that interest you.

Zite / Flipboard

(3 votes!)

Zite is now merged with Flipboard, a free news aggregator app that pulls in the day's top stories along with the articles that are trending in your social media feeds. Users can read and share articles that they like with others.

The Flipboard app is beautifully designed and I'll often use it to get my daily dose of news while waiting in line or relaxing on the couch.

URL: flipboard.com

Pricing: Free!

Charity Navigator

(2 votes!)

America's largest independent charity evaluator provides free ratings of the Financial Health and Accountability & Transparency of many charities.

URL: charitynavigator.org

Pricing: Free!

Forbes

(2 votes!)

A leading source for reliable business news and financial information.

URL: forbes.com

Pricing: Free online! (Or pay for the paper magazine subscription.)

Hacker News

(2 votes!)

Hacker News is a collection of tech news and interesting articles that can be voted up by users.

URL: news.ycombinator.com

Pricing: Free!

Reddit

(2 votes!)

Reddit's tagline is "The front page of the Internet." The most interesting and engaging articles make their way to the top of the various category pages through the community's voting and comments.

URL: reddit.com

Pricing: Free!

Circa - Get a briefing on the day's top stories in just minutes with this free smartphone app.

GiveWell - In-depth research into charities worldwide so you can make sure more of you money goes to support the causes you care most about.

InkDrop - English language newspapers from around the world for a fresh perspective on world events.

McKinsey Insights - The free McKinsey mobile app curates the best and most relevant news and stories for your business and industry.

Newsle - Never miss an article about someone who matters to you. When your friends & colleagues make the news, we make sure you know.

NewsStand - A collection of all the top news publications on your iOS device.

NYTimes - Stay up to date with "all the news that's fit to print" from around the world and around the corner.

Politico - A print and digital newspaper covering political news in the US.

Pulse.me - Now owned by LinkedIn, Pulse is a free news app with stories tailored to your interested based on what's popular and relevant to others in your network.

SEC.gov - SEC.gov is a free resource that provides information to protect businesses and individuals. They insure that investors are protected, markets are fair and orderly, and capital formation is facilitated.

Zillow - The web's leading source for local property values, homes for sales, and available rentals near your.

Outsourcing Resources

Sooner or later, every entrepreneur reaches the limit of their own capacity – either in terms of their skills or in terms of the hours in a day. When that happens, it's time to get help and build a team if they want to continue to grow.

These are the top outsourcing resources named, and you might be surprised at how affordable some of the options are, along with the variety of tasks you might be able to get off your plate.

Fiverr

(12 votes!)

Fiverr is a marketplace for goods and services all starting at just $5, and you'll be surprised by what you can get done for that price. Even though the site is somewhat known for the silly tasks (prank calls, impressions, costumed-dances, etc.), you can also get a ton of useful work done here as well.

I've used Fiverr for quick graphic design work, ebook covers, article writing, video intros, website tweaks, proofreading, my podcast voiceover intro, and even tax advice. There are more than 3 million gigs to choose from so odds are you can find someone with the skills you need.

Today, Fiverr is typically my first stop when I have a new micro-outsourcing project in mind. I'll do a search for what I need, and make sure to sort by "High Rating." I look for sellers who have a history of excellent feedback and have achieved either the Level 2 or Top-Rated Seller ranking, which indicates they have a strong track record on Fiverr and take their business seriously.

The thing to remember with Fiverr though is to align your expectations with the price tag. It's true, I've had some *amazing* work done there, but I've also had some pretty crappy work done too. Have fun with it, be patient, and when you find a great seller, be good to them and keep sending business their way.

URL: fiverr.com

Pricing: All "gigs" start at $5, but you can add-on extra services as needed for faster delivery, enhanced features, or other customization.

99designs

(4 votes!)

99designs specializes in crowdsourced graphic design for logos, websites, advertising, product packaging and more. How it works is you submit your design "spec," including the colors and styles you like along with some information about your company and brand, and an army of designers from around the world gets to work creating concepts for you.

It's a winner-take-all system, where all the designers are hoping they're the one you select from the crowd. The advantage of 99designs is you have access to several different designers with their different tastes and backgrounds, instead of hiring just one.

Naturally, the number of entries for each design contest varies by the size of the prize – the bigger the pot, the more designs you'll have to choose from. At the low end, you might get 30 different submissions, and higher-priced contests can earn 100 entries or more.

URL: 99designs.com

Pricing: Logo design services start at $299; website design from $599.

Elance

(3 votes!)

Hire a freelancer for any industry, field or skilled trade. Elance is free to join and post jobs or view profiles, and you can workers for project-based, part-time, or full-time engagements. There is a virtual workroom to track hours and a huge selection of talent at competitive rates.

I've had my best success in finding long-term virtual hires on Elance, but have been burned pretty badly by some smooth-talking web developers as well, so it goes both ways.

Fancy Hands

(2 votes!)

Fancy Hands is a task-based outsourcing company that makes personal assistance efficient and affordable for everyone. The assistants are all based in the US and can handle virtual and phone-related tasks that take up to 15 minutes.

Over the past couple years, I've become somewhat addicted to Fancy Hands and it's a very empowering feeling to have a team of assistants "on call" to deal with the tasks you don't want to or don't have time for.

You can submit tasks via email, phone, online, or from their smartphone app. I have them do things like check in for my Southwest flights, resize images, research various companies, proofread blog posts, make phone calls, and do data entry.

In fact, Fancy Hands was instrumental in compiling the information for this book!

URL: fancyhands.com

Pricing: $29.99 for 5 tasks per month; $49.99 for 15 tasks per month; $149.99 for 50 tasks per month. Unused tasks rollover month-to-month.

Freelancer.com

(2 votes!)

Freelancer.com is a global marketplace to find freelance talent for just about any kind of virtual job you need done. There is a huge database of talent available with skills that include web development, copywriting, administrative support, graphic design, bookkeeping, database maintenance, and more.

It's free to setup a profile, post a job, and select the service provider you need from the huge database of talent available.

URL: freelancer.com

Pricing: It's free to post a job, and freelancer rates vary based on the work you need done.

Task Rabbit

(2 votes!)

Task Rabbit is an on-demand errand-running service that also facilitates virtual work. You can outsource household chores or skilled tasks based on what you need done. Task Rabbit operates in select cities across the country but is growing quickly.

You can put your micro-job up for bid, and hire qualified respondents. Their screening process and review system makes sure that only the best assistants make it through.

Companies use Task Rabbit to fill temporary positions or to staff events, while busy individuals might find this local help useful for tasks like picking up dry cleaning or waiting in line for the latest iPhone.

URL: taskrabbit.com

Pricing: Task Rabbit pricing varies based on the task, but generally starts around $12 an hour.

Call Ruby - A US-based call answering / virtual receptionist service. Priced from $239 per month.

DesignCrowd - Similar in concept to 99designs, with logo design services starting at $99.

iWriter - If you need help keeping up with creating content for your blog or other writing, iWriter can help get it done with affordable rates starting at $1.25 per article.

Mechanical Turk - Crowdsourcing tool for data entry tasks or gathering cheap human feedback. Pricing starts at 1.5 cents per task.

oDesk - Browse a huge database of talented freelancers ready to perform the services you need at competitive rates.

Squadhelp - Crowdsourced contests for graphic designs, business names, viral videos, and more.

TextBroker - Customized writing at competitive prices – as little as $0.03 per word. You can place your request so that any registered freelancer could write it or choose to have a specific writer who specializes in the particular topic you need the article written about.

VirtualAssistantAssistant.com - The web's leading directory and review platform of virtual assistant and outsourcing companies.

WP Curve - Unlimited small WordPress tweaks and customizations for $69 per month.

Zirtual - Balance your work life and delegate tasks without the responsibility of hiring a new employee. Select a "Zirtual Assistant" for anywhere between 8 and 55 hours of assistance per month. You deal with the same dedicated, US-based assistant so the quality of service is consistent. Plans start at $199.00 per month and come with a 2-week free trial.

Productivity Tools

We all strive to be more productive in our work lives. There never seems to be enough hours in the day!

Volumes have been written on how to be a more productive person, with suggestions ranging from getting up earlier to eliminating your to-do list entirely, but the real secret is to find a "system" that works for you.

Only you can decide which productivity tools have a place in your daily life and which ones will cost more time than they save.

Evernote

(16 votes!)

Create an "external brain," and share and sync notes and files in the cloud with free and paid versions.

Any flash of inspiration can be saved in Evernote. All you need to do is to create a notebook and save the notes in there. The tool has numerous features, including sharing, file attachments, reminders, and voice memos. You can even scan text in a photo using Optical Character Recognition technology and access your notes when you're offline.

The Evernote web clipper lets you can save articles or other important links. Essentially, Evernote gives you a centralized depository for your ideas so they don't clutter up your brain. You know they'll be kept safe and accessible from any device, so you can save them to the app and go about your day, revisiting them at a time convenient to you.

URL: evernote.com

Pricing: The Basic Evernote plan is free. Evernote Premium is $5 per month and has additional features like 1 GB of monthly upload capacity and an increased max note size of 100 MB.

Wunderlist

(8 votes!)

Wunderlist helps manage tasks with to-do lists. Entrepreneurs and other productivity junkies can create a list of groupings and under each grouping, a list of tasks.

The Wunderlist system works in the cloud and syncs to all your devices, and you can share task lists with other members of your team as well.

URL: wunderlist.com

Pricing: Free and premium plans available.

WorkFlowy

(7 votes!)

WorkFlowy is a free tool to organize your ideas, lists, notes, plans, brainstorms, and workflows. It doesn't have all the bells and whistles that Evernote has, but many users swear by the simple interface and ease of use.

URL: workflowy.com

Pricing: Free!

IFTTT

(6 votes!)

Use IFTTT to create automated *If This, Then That* "recipes" to streamline events and become a productivity ninja. The service integrates with dozens of other online platforms including, Dropbox, Twitter, Evernote, Gmail, Google Calendar, WordPress, Text messaging, and more.

I have a handful of recipes set up, but need to spend some more time diving into the popular formulas to see how other people are using IFTTT.

So far, I have one that automatically saves my iPhone pics to Dropbox, one that sets up a reminder email with NudgeMail, and one that automatically adds each new WordPress post on my site to my Buffer account.

URL: ifttt.com

Pricing: Free!

Zapier

(6 votes!)

Zapier connects and automates applications with custom-defined recipes and rules, like IFTTT but more business-focused.

URL: zapier.com

Pricing: Pricing ranges from free to $99 per month.

Lift.Do

(4 votes!)

Lift.Do is a simple free goal-tracking app to keep you on track and keep you motivated. You can add one or more goals into the app, get daily reminders, and make notes about your progress.

Lift goals can be shared with other users with the same or similar goals, or you can chose to make yours private.

URL: lift.do

Pricing: Free!

RescueTime

(4 votes!)

Find your ideal work-life balance by showing you where you're spending the most time online and on your computer. Try to improve your percentage of productive time each week.

URL: rescuetime.com

Pricing: Free and premium plans are available.

TextExpander

(4 votes!)

The Auto TextExpander Chrome browser plugin allows you to create custom keyboard shortcuts that result in fully formed sentences, paragraphs, or other text.

I feel like a serious productivity ninja when I use this tool! For instance, you might set "hbd" to type out "Happy Birthday!"

I have a couple dozen shortcuts set up for things I found myself commonly typing out, such as introductory notes to clients, meeting invitations, and template-driven recommendations.

URL: The URL is ugly, so just Google "Auto TextExpander for Chrome."

Pricing: Free!

Time Doctor

(4 votes!)

Time Doctor tracks time to increase productivity and gives you detailed reports of how you and your team are spending your working hours. Friendly pop-up reminders help keep you on task and working toward your goals.

You can also use this tool to track the time of virtual assistants or other members on your team.

URL: timedoctor.com

Pricing: Time Doctor is free for personal use and $12 per month for teams of up to 3 people.

Amazon.com and Amazon Prime

(3 votes!)

Get free 2-day shipping on millions of items at the world's largest store with a $99 annual Amazon Prime membership, plus access to streaming TV shows, movies, and more.

The reason this is filed under Productivity is because Amazon saves me from running unnecessary errands; I just order from them and the item shows up on my doorstep two days later.

Focus@will

(3 votes!)

Focus@will provides neuroscience-based music channels to increase attention up to 400%.

URL: focusatwill.com

Pricing: They have both free and paid versions starting at $5.99 per month.

LastPass

(3 votes!)

A secure password management service. I rely on LastPass to remember all my passwords and it's a huge time and brain-space saver. You can also use it to securely share passwords with other members of your team, without revealing the actual password, and revoke access at any time.

URL: lastpass.com

Pricing: Free and premium plans are available.

MySpeed

(3 votes!)

MySpeed is software that speeds up online videos. If you've ever been frustrated by slow-talking videos on YouTube or Udemy, this is for you!

URL: enounce.com/myspeed

Pricing: $30.

StayFocusd

(3 votes!)

StayFocusd is a free Chrome browser extension that helps you block time-killing websites so you can stay on task and get more done. It is configurable to your personal needs but the basic premise is to "hand over your keys" to your computer because you can't be trusted to drive yourself.

After the pre-allotted time for your off-limit sites is up, the app will lock you out for the rest of the day.

The StayFocusd website is a one-page site that simply asks, "Shouldn't you be working?"

URL: stayfocusd.com

Pricing: Free, but donations are appreciated.

1Password

(2 votes!)

1Password creates strong, unique passwords for all of your sites and logs you in with a single master password. It's simple, convenient security.

URL: 1password.com

Pricing: $49.99.

Breevy

(2 votes!)

Breevy is a text expander and AutoText text replacement program that helps you type faster and more accurately by allowing you to abbreviate long words and phrases with your own custom keyboard shortcuts.

URL: 16software.com/breevy

Pricing: $34.95 after 30-day free trial.

Freedom

(2 votes!)

Freedom for Mac, Windows, and Android shuts off your computer's Internet access so you can focus without distractions.

URL: macfreedom.com

Pricing: The software is $10.

Google Chrome

(2 votes!)

Chrome is Google's free web browser that promises a fast and secure online experience. I made the switch from Firefox a few years ago and haven't looked back.

The best part about Chrome is their ever-growing library of extensions. Here are 10 of my favorites.

URL: chrome.com

Pricing: Free!

Google Keep

(2 votes!)

Google Keep is Google's alternative to Evernote. The service can be accessed through Google Drive or by downloading the free Android App.

With Keep, you can find printed text in photos, set where new items go, and add your own voice memos.

There is an option to use different color for each type of note, but lacks some sharing and grouping capabilities of rival services.

URL: keep.google.com

Pricing: Free!

Mindjet

(2 votes!)

Mindjet is used by business as a platform for enterprise innovation. It may not be best suited to sole proprietors and other small businesses, but Mindjet is used in many Fortune 500 companies and has a 10+ year legacy in the corporate world.

Mindjet helps companies and teams manage their ideas, projects, and create innovation instead of just following the status quo. It has a visual layout that organizes all your documents in one location, making Mindjet a popular choice to map out brainstorming, organize information, and plan complex projects.

Online sharing and other features are built-in.

URL: mindjet.com

Pricing: Pricing starts at $349.

OmniFocus

(2 votes!)

OmniFocus is a Mac, iPhone, and iPad app born from the *Getting Things Done* methodology that quickly captures your thoughts and ideas to store, manage, and help you process them into actionable to-do items.

One cool point of differentiation from other similar apps is the Perspective feature, which filters your high-priority, important information when you need it. OmniFocus is highly customizable so you can use it in the way that makes the most sense to you.

URL: omnigroup.com/omnifocus

Pricing: An OmniFocus Individual License is $79.99 and a Family License is $119.99.

Readability

(2 votes!)

Readability is a free tool to turn any web page into a clean view for reading now or later on your computer, smartphone, or tablet. You can adjust the text to different styles and sizes and even change the background color.

You can use the "Top Read" list to discover new content and use the built-in sharing features to let friends and followers know about great articles.

URL: readability.com

Pricing: Free!

Remember the Milk

(2 votes!)

Remember the Milk is a simple task management app for Android and iOS. You can add tasks quickly and make use of smart keyboard shortcuts to gain even more speed.

Search for previously-added tasks, review tasks by location, or receive reminders via email, text or instant messenger.

URL: rememberthemilk.com

Pricing: Remember the Milk has a free basic version and a Pro version for $25 per year that unlocks additional features.

Self Control

(2 votes!)

Self Control is a free Mac application that blocks distracting websites.

It lets you block your own access to distracting websites, your mail servers, or anything else you do not want to use for a custom period of time – and it means business; even if you restart your computer or delete the application, you will still be unable to have access.

If you think Facebook and Twitter are consuming too much of your productive time, then this can be the right self-imposed "detox diet" plan for you or your company.

URL: selfcontrolapp.com

Pricing: Free!

Simpleology

(2 votes!)

Simpleology keeps you on track and shortens that gap between where you are and where you want to be. Free and premium versions are available.

Siri

(2 votes!)

Siri is the built-in virtual assistant on newer models of the iPhone. She lets you use your voice to send messages, schedule meetings, place phone calls, and more.

I've been using Siri more and more lately – to set up reminders ("Siri, remind me to move my car at 7:30."), or to find out the score of the Mariners game ("Siri, are the Mariners winning?"). She's awesome!

Android peeps can use a similar virtual assistant tool like Speaktoit.

URL: apple.com/ios/siri

Pricing: Free with iPhone purchase.

Things

(2 votes!)

Things is a professional task management app for Mac, iPhone, and iPad. Information syncs between devices so you can use the same consistent interface at home, at the office, or on the road.

URL: culturedcode.com/things

Pricing: $50.

Todoist

(2 votes!)

Keep track and access your top priority tasks from anywhere.

URL: todoist.com

Pricing: Free and premium versions are available.

ActionAlly - A Mac application to help you consistently take action on your most important work. Priced at $37 after a 7-day free trial.

ActiveWords - Like the Text Expander for Chrome extension I'm in love with, except for desktop applications as well. They have free and paid versions.

Android - Google's operating system for tablets, smartphones, and apps got a vote from Guy Kawasaki.

Anti-Social - Block access to social media sites for $15.

Captio - Email yourself with just one tap. The app is $1.99.

CheckVist - Capture ideas, create checklists, and manage tasks. Free and paid versions are available.

ClipX - A simple free program that allows your Windows clipboard to hold up to 1024 items, instead of just one.

CopyClip - CopyClip is a simple and efficient clipboard manager for Mac.

E.ggtimer.com - Free, simple web-based timer application.

EasilyDo - A virtual personal assistant app for iOS, Android, and Gmail to make you more productive and connected. It's an integrated productivity tool with no to-do lists, no digging, and no switching back and forth between applications. Get a free basic account or go premium and unlock additional features for as little as $4.99 a month.

FastEver Snap - A camera app that quickly sends photos to Evernote, with smart file size compression to reduce storage space. Priced at $1.99 in iTunes.

FlyCut - Free clipboard manager for Mac.

Freckle - Freckle is a time tracker that helps you remember to track your time. It's priced starting at $49 a month. (I've used an app called Toggl.com instead, described below.)

FreeMind - Like all mind maps, FreeMind gives you the flexibility to organize thoughts on a page as they connect to each other and to the larger picture

Futureme.org - Use this free service to write a letter to your future self to remind yourself of important lessons you don't want to forget.

Gingko App - Whether you're organizing your research, strategizing your business, or just clearing your mind, Gingko gives you a place to clarify your thoughts.

HiFutureSelf - HiFutureSelf is a free app that brings the ease of text messaging to setting up alerts and reminders. With as few as two taps you can set up reminders for your daily routine.

iBrainstorm - iBrainstorm is a free alternative to Evernote. Notes can be taken whenever they are needed and shared with others.

iDoneThis - iDoneThis is a simple tool that sends you an email each day asking what you got done. You simply type up a reply and hit send and the service records you answers.

It helps keep you accountable, since you know the email is coming, and can also be used to keep tabs on your team members' daily progress as well. Free for individuals, $5 per user per month for teams.

iJot - An iPhone app that lets you create and share handwritten notes using your finger as the pen.

InkPad - InkPad is another free note-taking app.

irunurun - A simple performance and accountability system for individuals or teams. Free and premium versions are available.

iThoughtsHD - iThoughtsHD provides a mind-mapping service to increase creativity and productive brainstorming opportunities. Available for $9.99 on iTunes.

jitouch - Create multi-touch gestures for you Mac touchpad to get around much faster. Priced at $7.99 after free trial.

KanbanFlow - KanbanFlow is a free resource for businesses and individuals to help increase workflow and productivity. It boosts your personal or team productivity through visual aids and time management tools.

KeePass - KeePass is a free open source password manager, which helps you to manage your passwords in a secure way.

Kindle Highlights - Kindle Highlights can be synced up with a device connected with Amazon for free to show passages or sentences that have been highlighted for future reference.

Kona - Kona helps organize information, share data between users, and increase productivity. Available for free for individuals and $10 per month per user for groups.

Momentum - Momentum is a free Chrome extension that replaces the default new browser tab with a personal dashboard featuring to-do items, weather, beautiful pictures, and inspirational quotes.

Mind Meister - Mind Meister inspires creativity through mind mapping, brainstorming, and collaborating with others, with free and premium subscriptions available.

Mindomo - Mindomo will help you to brainstorm and mind map successful ideas. Free and premium plans are available.

NoteApp - This note-taking app has both free and paid versions.

NVALT - NValt is a free service that takes notes quickly and effortlessly using just your keyboard.

OneTab - Free browser extension to help your Chrome or Firefox browser run with less memory by keeping your common tabs in a dropdown list.

PaperKarma - This free app helps reduce clutter in your physical mailbox by opting out of junk mail lists. Just snap a picture of the envelope and the app takes care of the rest.

Phrase Express (PC) - Phrase Express is a text expander software for PC users. It's free for personal use.

PopClip - PopClip appears when you select text with your mouse on your Mac. Instantly copy & paste, and access actions like search, spelling, dictionary and over 100 more. Priced at $4.99 after free trial.

RoboForm - RoboForm is a top-rated password management tool that costs $9.95/year.

TeuxDeux - TeuxDeux helps organize your to-do list and get things done. Priced at $2 - $3 per month.

Text-Expander - Keyboard shortcut software for Mac. $35.

The Brain - TheBrain is a mind mapping software that aids brainstorming and thought organization. Pricing starts at $15 per month.

Toggl - Toggl's free time tracking software helps keep you on task and record how much time you spend in each area of your business.

TomatoTimer – The TomatoTimer is a free, easy to use, flexible Pomodoro Technique timer.

Tomorrow.do - A simple free to-do list app to kill procrastination.

VirtualPostMail - Get a real US address to receive postal mail. View your mail online without forwarding. Manage your postal mail no matter where in the world you live – perfect for digital nomads and long-term travelers. Pricing from $5 - $30 per month.

Voice Memo - Record voice messages to yourself while on the go. I use the built-in free version on my iPhone sometimes while I'm driving, and it's also available as a standalone iPad app for $0.99.

Social Media Resources

Social media is a huge part of our online lives both for personal and business use. These resources represent an opportunity to connect with customers and peers in open and honest ways, share helpful and valuable content, and promote your product or service offerings.

LinkedIn

(15 votes!)

I was surprised to see LinkedIn as the most-recommended social media resource, but that's a strong indicator it is an overlooked tool for entrepreneurs. You can use LinkedIn to highlight your accomplishments, share your content, and connect with other professionals.

LinkedIn pages tend to rank highly in Google if someone is searching your name, so it's important to put your best foot forward on your profile. That means reaching the 500+ connection mark, building out an up-to-date resume, sharing your publications, and soliciting recommendations and endorsements.

You can also use LinkedIn groups to make connections with like-minded people and to help share your content.

URL: linkedin.com

Pricing: LinkedIn is a free social network, but premium accounts unlock advanced features and functionality from $23.99 per month.

Buffer

(11 votes!)

Buffer helps you manage multiple social media accounts at once. You can quickly schedule content from anywhere on the web, collaborate with team members, and analyze rich statistics on how your posts perform.

I've been using Buffer for the last several months to share content on Twitter throughout the week and think it's pretty awesome. This allows me to share the articles I like and think my followers will find valuable, spread out over the week, while still doing all my blog reading in one or two batches.

URL: bufferapp.com

Pricing: Buffer has a free version and an "Awesome" plan that costs $10 a month and allows for up to 12 social media accounts and up to 200 posts in your Buffer queue.

Facebook

(12 votes!)

Facebook is the world's most popular social network with over a billion members. Entrepreneurs can use Facebook to connect with new and old friends, share photos and videos, join groups with common interests, build a business network, and market their services.

With Facebook Custom Audiences, small businesses can target ads for people who are likely to be interested in that service or product they offer. The pricing varies depending on your budget and the options chosen.

I have a community page for Side Hustle Nation, am in several groups, and have logged in daily (often multiple times per day) for years, but I still feel like I'm only scratching the surface of what Facebook could be. Savvy small business owners are using the platform to generate leads and sales instead of a time-suck distraction.

One challenge facing Page owners is the diminishing organic reach their posts will have. Over time, Facebook limits the percentage of your fans who will see your content in their news feeds, even though they've "liked" your page to theoretically see those updates.

Still, Facebook is an important platform to at least have a presence so you can engage with your target customers in an environment they're familiar with.

URL: facebook.com

Pricing: Free!

HootSuite

(10 votes!)

Having a hard time keeping track and updating your social media accounts? HootSuite manages it all for you. Post to Facebook, Twitter, or Google+, simultaneously or individually, at the time you schedule.

Monitor the social pulse of your business from one central dashboard and track the engagement of your social media campaigns with easy-to-read reports.

URL: hootsuite.com

Pricing: Free and paid versions available. The Pro version is $8.99 per month and includes advanced features and functionality.

Twitter

(9 votes!)

Twitter was billed as a "microblogging" platform, with all posts limited to 140 characters, but it has become much more than that. Entrepreneurs can use Twitter to answer questions and demonstrate their expertise, interact with customers, share content and pictures, and connect with other interesting people.

I was a latecomer to Twitter, but in the past year I've connected with some awesome people through the service! It's great for informal introductions and networking. Are we connected?

URL: twitter.com

Pricing: Free!

Instagram

(6 votes!)

Use the free Instagram app to display products images, company advertisements, portfolio pieces, or simply your favorite images. In addition to still photos, Instagram supports 15 second video clips, which you can utilize to provide a quick message to clients, followers, or personal contacts.

URL: instagram.com

Pricing: Free!

YouTube

(5 votes!)

Upload videos and share them with the world for free. YouTube has become a popular online teacher with their huge database of "how-to" videos. You can also market your business and receive feedback or use it for fun and share memorable moments.

I've recently discovered the power of YouTube in syndicating audio content from my podcast there. It's just one more avenue of exposure for listeners/viewers to come in contact with your brand and message.

URL: youtube.com

Pricing: Free!

Pinterest

(4 votes!)

Choose from thousands of ideas or share your own (pin it!) on this image-centric social platform. Beautiful pictures and image-quotes tend to perform best, and since each image can link back to your site, Pinterest is an excellent traffic source.

If you aren't ready to share your work with the world, want to plan a surprise event, or keep track of personal "pin" lists (Christmas list, grocery shopping, business goals, etc.), you can create a Pinterest Secret Board.

URL: pinterest.com

Pricing: Free!

Quora

(4 votes!)

Quora is a question and answer site where you can gain exposure and social credit by writing thoughtful and helpful answers to people's questions. Your earned credits can be redeemed to "promote" certain questions and answers to reach a wider audience.

In general, the quality on Quora tends to be about a million times better than say, Yahoo Answers.

Quora ranks well in Google and can be a good place to build up your reputation as an expert on a certain topic.

URL: quora.com

Pricing: Free!

Google+

(3 votes!)

Google+ is Google's free social network. Even though the platform is growing larger every day, its future remains uncertain as it lags far behind rival Facebook. Users can upload their favorite photos, videos, quotes, book reviews, and more, and connect with colleagues and peers.

If you don't have one already, be sure to set up a Google+ for Business page because it can be an easy way to get additional exposure in the search results.

URL: plus.google.com

Pricing: Free!

PostPlanner

(2 votes!)

PostPlanner takes care of your Facebook marketing for you. All you have to do is create your posts, schedule them, and forget about them. Never waste spare moment adding posts to your pages.

Post Planner makes it easy to run a highly-engaged Facebook page by showing you the freshest trending content in your niche, proven pre-written status updates, and real-time analytics so you can post at the peak times.

URL: postplanner.com

Pricing: A basic version or PostPlanner is free, and premium plans start at $19 per month.

SocialOomph

(2 votes!)

Boost your social media productivity by easily scheduling updates, finding quality people to follow, and monitoring social media activity. Free and professional versions are available.

Click to Tweet - Craft pre-written tweets and share the link anywhere. Perfect for blog posts or asking people to share your material with one click via email. Free and premium versions are available. Lately I've been using a rival service called HrefShare.com, which has capability for other social networks beyond just Twitter.

Commun.It - Schedule your Twitter updates, monitor your account performance, and interact with your followers.

Crowdfire - Find targeted people to follow on Twitter or Instagram and see who doesn't follow you back. Free and premium versions are available.

Dribbble - Dribbble is "show and tell for designers," a place to promote, discover, and explore web, graphic, illustration, logo, and typography design.

Drip In - Schedule social media updates in a systematic campaign across several platforms.

Edgar - A social media management and scheduling tool.

Empire Avenue - Create a social profile and get rewarded as you discover content and people through missions.

List.ly - This free service helps bloggers, content creators, and publishers get discovered. Write a useful new list post and submit it to the site.

Ning - Ning is a scalable hosted platform that gives you the tools and expertise you need to build your own social network, publish, and share with your community, all in one place. Pricing from $25.

Prismatic - Prismatic is a free RSS feed social platform. You can stream your favorite feeds and read and share your opinion with others from around the world.

SlideShare - Use SlideShare to share awesome and effective presentations. Whether you're trying to share a concept, sell something, or report information, SlideShare is a great place to do it.

The site tends to rank well in Google and great presentations can generate a lot of viral buzz and referral traffic. You can embed links inside your pdf presentation files to drive visitors back to your site. Free and paid versions are available.

SMQueue - SMQueue helps keep you active and engaged on social media, without spending your whole day on Twitter and Facebook.

Social Crawlytics - Find out for free where your competitor's content is being shared and promoted.

SocialFlow.com - SocialFlow uses your social media accounts to improve your content and user engagement.

Spreecast - Spreecast is free video chatting software. You can chat with website members, colleagues, high profile individuals, family, and friends.

Sprout Social - Sprout Social is a social media management platform that doubles as Client Relations Management software. You can schedule your posts on Twitter, Facebook, Google+, etc., view analytics and monitor what people are saying about your brand, and send messages and keep track of conversations. Pricing starts at $59 per month after a 30-day free trial.

Tweet Old Post - Tweet Old Post is a free WordPress plugin that automatically tweets out your older content at regular intervals to breathe new life into your blog archives.

TwitterFeed - Twitterfeed is a utility that allows you to feed your content to Twitter and other social platforms, and track real-time performance. Free and premium plans area available.

Twuffer - Twuffer is a free tool that allows you to compose a list of future tweets, and schedule their release.

WhoTalking.com - Type in any keyword (your name, your company, your niche), and get real-time results to see who's talking about that topic online.

Team and Project Management Tools

As your team grows, so does your need for an intuitive system to communicate and get the work done together. These are the resources to help you manage your team and your projects efficiently and effectively.

Asana

(27 votes!)

Asana is a web-based project-management system, free for teams up to 15 members. Their tagline is "Teamwork without email," and it was the 2nd most-named resource in the study, after Google Docs / Google Drive.

For many entrepreneurs I talked to, Asana has become an integral part of their daily life. Users can set and assign tasks to themselves or other team members. All members can have access to the tasks and comment and update their progress as well.

The main idea is to save time by cutting down on meetings, status reports, and emails.

URL: asana.com

Pricing: Asana is free for teams of up to 15 members. Beyond that, premium plans start at $50 per month.

Basecamp

(20 votes!)

Basecamp is one of the best-known project management applications and has served millions of customers over the last

15+ years. The web-based software is intuitive and easy-to-use, making team collaboration simple and efficient.

The Basecamp experience centers on the Dashboard, a high-level summary of all business tasks and events that looks like a Facebook newsfeed. Users who aren't logged into the system regularly will receive email alerts on project and task updates.

All Basecamp plans allow for an unlimited number of team members, and include cloud-based data storage ranging from 3 GB to 500 GB.

URL: basecamp.com

Pricing: Subscriptions start at $20 per month, and they offer a 60-day free trial.

Trello

(20 votes!)

Trello is an online organizer, to-do list app, and team collaborator. It shares many similarities with Asana, but visual thinkers tend to prefer Trello as its interface uses boards and cards for organization.

The app can be used on Android, iPhone, iPad, Windows 8 Tablet, and your web browser.

URL: trello.com

Pricing: The basic version of Trello is available for free, with additional features and functionality starting at $45 per year.

Jing

(6 votes!)

Jing is a free screen recording software tool that lets you create screen-capture videos of up to 5 minutes at a time with a voiceover narration. I use it to share quick walkthrough instructional videos with my team.

Jing's software makes it very easy to upload to the cloud and share the URL with whoever needs to view the video; no big files to send via email.

URL: techsmith.com/jing

Pricing: Jing is free software and comes with 2 GB of free cloud storage to host your videos.

Slack

(6 votes!)

Slack is a communication tool that supports real-time messaging, archiving, and search for modern teams to help get you out of your inbox and get more done.

URL: slack.com

Pricing: A free plan is available, and premium access starts at less than $7 per user per month.

Podio

(5 votes!)

Podio manages and organizes the communication between team members to increase productivity.

What really sets Podio apart is how it puts people in control of their work tools, rather than the other way around. You decide how to structure your projects, teams, and workflows by creating your own workspaces and sharing them with relevant people. You also decide how to structure, create and present content and information that's linked to your work processes and interactions.

You do this by choosing from hundreds of Podio's specialized work apps or creating your own to help you get the job done. Podio aims to help eliminate the blind spots and bottlenecks found in other project management software.

URL: podio.com

Pricing: Podio is free for teams of up to 5 members, and then $9 per month per user beyond that.

15Five

(4 votes!)

15five is a communication tool to be used between managers and their employees. Employees write up to 15 minute weekly report that will take their manager 5 minutes to read.

The result is employees feeling more engaged and feeling like their voice is heard on a weekly basis, and managers save time by reading and providing feedback in one time and place. Everyone stays in touch with what's important.

The main idea of the application is that that the 15-minute constraint forces creativity and productivity. It's a fast and effective way to increase the internal communication of your team and unlock higher performance.

URL: 15five.com

Pricing: This service is $49 per month for the first ten users. For each additional user the price is $5. There is 30-day free trial.

Harvest

(2 votes!)

Harvest is a time-tracking application that's helpful for creating invoices for payments. It is mainly suitable for the service industry and other hourly contractors.

Harvest is can be set-up within seconds with no installation process to go through. Users can easily create invoices and send to recipients via email. The customers then can easily log into the application and make the payment. There are no limits to the number of customers a user can have.

There is one-click time entry and easy tracking from any PC, MAC, mobile, and through any social media tools, which is helpful for managing a team's work, time, and progress toward project milestones. You can filter billable, non-billable, employee or contractor hours and export them as reports to your desktop.

URL: getharvest.com

Pricing: Pricing for Harvest starts at $12 per month for up to 3 users. There is a 30-day free trial on all accounts.

Lucidchart

(2 votes!)

Lucidchart is a sleek wireframing and flow chart tool to help visually communicate with your team. This is very useful to diagram processes or sales funnels, collaborate on changes, and share updates with everyone on the project.

URL: lucidchart.com

Pricing: Free for single users. Premium plans start at $40 per year.

TeamworkPM

(2 votes!)

TeamworkPM is an online project and team management site.

A list of projects on the left-hand side of the page allows you to easily select from all your projects, view the latest tasks and discussions, and measure your progress. Users enjoy the thoughtful interface that easily allows you to switch between projects and the helpful dashboard with informative overview tabs.

URL: teamwork.com

Pricing: Pricing for TeamworkPM ranges from $12 - $149 per month.

Hubstaff - Time tracking software with screenshots. Free and premium plans are available.

Huddle - Huddle increases business productivity with team collaboration and file sharing. Subscriptions are available at $20 per user per month.

Jira - Plan, track, and manage your projects with Jira's team organization software, starting at $10 per month.

Kanban Tool - Visual project management tool to increase team performance.

LeanKit - Visualize your processes and collaborate more effectively with LeanKit, a highly flexible platform designed for the practical implementation of Kanban. Free and premium versions are available.

Live Plan - Business planning software for $20 per month.

Mavenlink - Mavenlink provides online product and team management tools. It starts at $8 per user per month.

Mural.ly - Visual collaboration for creative teams.

Redbooth (formerly Teambox) - Online project management software to facilitate collaboration and team productivity. Free for up to 5 users.

SweetProcess - Stop spending time on repetitive tasks. Get them documented and out of your head, so someone else can do them. Pricing starts at $29 per month.

Workstack - Workstack is a Basecamp add-on that helps you to manage the priorities and workflow of each person in your team, all from a single interactive calendar view. Pricing from $6.99 per month with a 30-day free trial.

Wrike - Wrike provides a free project management and planning tool.

Yammer - Yammer helps facilitate communication within organizations. Free and premium versions are available.

Travel Resources

Whether you travel for business, pleasure, or both, these resources can help you make the most of your experience. For me, having the freedom and flexibility to travel and work from anywhere is one of the biggest perks of being self-employed.

Airbnb

(3 votes!)

Airbnb is a peer-to-peer lodging network that's disrupting the hotel industry. You can rent overnight stays from individuals instead of hotels, with the opportunity to have more space, save money, and even meet interesting hosts.

Some Airbnb places give you full run of the house or apartment, and in other cases you'll be in the spare bedroom with your hosts under the same roof. Before booking, you can check out pictures and reviews from previous guests.

And of course on the flip side, Airbnb represents a unique opportunity to turn your extra space into extra cash each month by hosting travelers from all around the world.

URL: airbnb.com

Pricing: Pricing varies based on location and amenities, but generally ranges from $50-200 per night.

Bonus: Get $25 off your first stay by signing up through sidehustlenation.com/airbnb.

TripIt

(3 votes!)

If you are going to be traveling, it is a good idea to be prepared. TripIt is an all-in-one travel organizer; forward your confirmation emails to plans@tripit.com and the system will build out your personalized itinerary that you can access from anywhere.

You can also share your arrivals on social media to connect with members of your network who might be in the same city.

URL: tripit.com

Pricing: TripIt is free to use, but a pro version ($49 per year) unlocks advanced features like mobile alerts and the ability to automatically share your itinerary with an "Inner Circle."

AroundMe

(2 votes!)

AroundMe is a free app that uses your smartphone's GPS to show you the nearby restaurants, stores, gas stations, cafes, hotels, banks, and more.

You can search for a specific store (eg. "starbucks") or browse the different categories if you're looking to discover something new.

URL: aroundmeapp.com

Pricing: Free! Upgrade to the ad-free version for $2.99.

Bed Bug Registry - No one wants to have creepy crawlies in their bed, but it can be a definite concern when traveling. Bed Bug Registry shows you where bed bugs have been found before.

CruiseSheet - Book unpublished cruise deals at big savings.

DogVacay - When owners go on vacation, sometimes pets can't go too. That's where DogVacay comes in. They match up pets with pet-sitters in a peer-to-peer network as an alternative to dog boarding or kennels. Think Airbnb, but for dogs! Generally the prices start at $20 per night.

Executive Planet - Essential business etiquette and culture guides for international travel.

Feastly - Feastly can be a great option for a fun and interesting night out. Chefs make meals in their homes and "feasters" can search for meals being cooked nearby and join the feast for a fee specified by the host.

Galileo - The free Galileo map app uses your GPS instead of a cell signal so you can use it while you're traveling internationally without incurring data charges.

Karma - Portable 4G LTE WiFi hotspot device with no monthly subscription. Priced at $149 for the device, and you pay for the data you use as you go.

RelayRides - Rent cars from RelayRides' nationwide car sharing marketplace or make money by renting out your car. The rates vary based on the type of care you're renting.

Startuptravels - Find startup communities and inspiring entrepreneurs all around the world as you travel.

Uber - Uber is a transportation resource that connects people with drivers. Fares vary based on time of day, demand, and travel distance.

Bonus: Get your first Uber ride free (up to $20) with code NICKL678!

VRBO - Perfect for large families and groups traveling together, Vacation Rental by Owner is a database of vacation properties you can stay at during your trip as an alternative to a traditional hotel.

Websites, Blogs, and Podcasts

Entrepreneurs read blogs and listen to podcasts to stay on top of industry news and events, as well as to learn and gain inspiration from their peers.

I aggregate my blog reading into Feedly (mentioned in the Education category) and browse the new posts every couple days. It's nice to have one central location to consume the content and get useful and actionable advice from the authors I follow.

From Feedly, I can also add posts to my Buffer for social sharing (mentioned in the Social Media category) and link directly to the article to leave a comment.

And for podcasts, I'm subscribed to a few favorite shows so they automatically download to my phone. That way they're ready to go when I'm off to the gym, walking the dog, or going for a drive.

These were the blogs and podcasts mentioned.

Entrepreneur on Fire

(4 votes!)

Your daily dose of entrepreneurial inspiration in podcast and blog form.

URL: eofire.com

Pricing: Free!

Springwise

(2 votes!)

Your essential daily fix of inspiring innovations and entrepreneurial ideas.

URL: springwise.com

Pricing: Free access and premium subscriptions are available.

AVC.com - The blog of venture capitalist Fred Wilson, discussing all things start-ups.

BrianTracy.com - The blog of bestselling author Brian Tracy. (*Eat That Frog!*, *Goals!*, *No Excuses!*, and more.)

Copyblogger.com - Brian Clark's hugely popular blog about blogging and content marketing.

DigitalBookWorld.com - This resource for modern authors shares the latest news, trends, strategies, and information on digital book publishing and marketing.

Fstoppers.com - A blog for aspiring and professional photographers.

GrowthHackers.com - A community of growth-minded marketers sharing useful content.

Hardcore History - Well-researched and entertaining historical storytelling by Dan Carlin. Available as a free podcast with archives for purchase.

LessDoing.com - A blog and podcast by Ari Meisel on becoming the most effective version of yourself physically and mentally through optimization, automation, and outsourcing.

Mixergy - Andrew Warner's been interviewing high-performing entrepreneurs since before it was cool.

Monday Morning Memo - Weekly email newsletter (on Mondays, surprise!) on marketing, advertising, sales, and other philosophical ramblings.

NathanBarry.com - The blog of author and app designer Nathan Barry, discussing online marketing, product launches, pricing strategy, and more.

PauloCoelhoBlog.com - The blog of bestselling author Paulo Coelho (*The Alchemist*), discussing creativity, positivity, and more.

Positively Positive - Daily affirmations, positive news, and uplifting stories.

RobinSharma.com - One of the world's most trusted leadership advisors, helping people in organizations lead regardless of their title.

Seth Godin's Blog - Daily updates from one of the most influential marketing thought-leaders out there.

Smart Passive Income - The blog of online entrepreneur Pat Flynn, discussing online business, blogging, marketing, podcasting, and more.

SocialMediaExaminer.com - Social media marketing news, tips, case studies, and more.

Start With Why - From author Simon Sinek, inspiring people to do the work that inspires them.

Steven Pressfield's Blog - The blog of author of *The War of Art, Turning Pro*, and more.

Suitcase Entrepreneur - A blog, podcast, and community for people building location-independent businesses. Founded by Natalie Sisson.

Wait But Why - Fascinating infographics on a broad range of topics.

Wrap Up

There you have it! The top 500+ tools named by today's top entrepreneurs.

Armed with these resources, I'm confident you'll be able to run a smarter, faster, more profitable business than ever before.

What did we miss?

Do you have a favorite tool or resource that wasn't listed? Send me a note (nick@sidehustlenation.com) and I'll include it in the next edition!

Contributors

This book would not have been possible without the tremendous contributions from more than 800 awesome entrepreneurs. Contributors are sorted alphabetically by first name.

Aaron Holland, Aaron Kahlow, Aaron Marcus, Aaron Schwartz, Aaron Walker, Aaron Young, Abbie Unger, Abel James, Ace Chapman, Adam Braun, Adam Franklin, Adam Lieb, Adam Markowitz, Adam Urbanski, Aigerim Shorman, AJ Leon, AJ Roberts, Akshay Nanavati, Alan Arlt, Alex Barker, Alex Genadinik, Alex Harris, Alex McClafferty, Alex Rodriguez, Alexandra Franzen, Alexis Grant, Alexis Neely, Alicia Rittenhouse, Alison Pena, Allon Caidar, Alyssa Dazet, Amanda Abella, Amanda Berlin, Amanda Pekoe, Amanda Weathersby, Amber Ludwig, Amber McCue, Amy Clover, Amy Kauffman, Andrea Vahl, Andrea Waltz, Andreea Ayers, Andrew Henderson, Andrew McCauley, Andrew Warner, Andrew Youderian, Andrew Zirkin, Andy Drish, Andy Murphy, Andy Stager, Andy Traub, Andy Wilson, Angela Watson, Anna Akbari, Anthony Vennare, Antonio Centeno, Antony Rousseliotakis, Apparao Karri, April Perry, Ari Meisel, Arnold Sanchez, Art Pollard, Ash Ambirge, Athena Yap, Aubrey Marcus, Aunia Kahn, Austin Muhs.

Barbara Anne Rose, Bea Arthur, Becky McKinnell, Becky Robinson, Ben Greenfield, Ben Newman, Ben Sardella, Benny Hsu, Bernadette Jiwa, Beth Davis, Beth Hayden, Beth Millman, Betsy and Warren Talbot, Bill Baren, Bill Brown, Bill Clerico, Bill Glaser, Bill Schley, Bill Seaver, Billy Murphy, Blake Andrews, Bo Eason, Bob Burg, Bob Caspe, Brad Costanzo, Brad Spencer, Braden Kelley, Brandee Sweesy, Brandon Allen, Brandon Epstein, Branko Cerny, Brant Cooper,

Breanden Beneschott, Brendon Sinclair, Brent Gleeson, Brenton Hayden, Brett Campbell, Brett Kelly, Brian Bagnall, Brian Church, Brian Horn, Brian Kurtz, Brian Moran, Brian Solis, Brian Swichkow, Brian Tracy, Bryan Harris, Bryan Kelly, Bryan Kreuzberger, Bryan Miles, Bryan Orr, Bryn Miyahara, Budi Voogt.

Caelen King, Caleb Bacon, Cameron Herold, Carl Heaton, Carl Mattiola, Carlos Miceli, Carol Cain, Carrie Contey, Carrie Green, Carter Thomas, Casey Zeman, Catherine Hoke, Caue Suplicy, Cevin Ormond, Chad Hamzeh, Chad Lawie, Chandler Bolt, Charles Friedman, Charlie Gilkey, Charlie McDermott, Charlie Megan, Charlie Poznek, Chase Reeves, Chemda, Cheryl Snapp Conner, Chris Brogan, Chris Ducker, Chris Evans, Chris Farrell, Chris Hawker, Chris Hogan, Chris Kilbourn, Chris LoCurto, Chris Ovitz, Chris Taylor, Christie Mims, Christina Daves, Christof Appel, Christopher Kelly, Claire Lew, Clay Clark, Clint Arthur, Conrad Egusa, Corbett Barr, Corey Poirier, Corey Vagos, Corey Wadden, Corrina Gordon-Barnes, Cory Boatright, Courtney McKenzie, Croix Sather, Cynthia Sanchez, Cynthia Schames.

Dale Partridge, Dale Stephens, Damian Thompson, Dan Andrews, Dan Corkill, Dan Goldman, Dan Granger, Dan Martell, Dan Miller, Dan Norris, Dan Pena, Dan Pink, Dan R. Morris, Dan Schawbel, Dana Pepper, Dana Wilde, Daniel Bailey, Daniel DiPiazza, Daniel Faggella, Daniel Himel, Daniel J. Lewis, Daniel Radcliffe, Danielle Laporte, Danielle Watson, Danny Flood, Danny Iny, Darren LaCroix, Darryl Lyons, Darwin Carlisle, Daryl Urbanski, Dave Arnold, Dave Austin, Dave Crenshaw, Dave Delaney, Dave Jackson, Dave Kerpen, Dave Ortiz, Dave Schneider, Dave Taylor, David Bradford, David Craige, David Elliott, David Friend, David Fugate, David Hassell, David Hutcherson, David Kadavy, David Long, David

McKeegan, David Meerman Scott, David Newman, David Sturt, David Wood, Davyeon Ross, Dawn Fotopulos, Dayne Shuda, Deacon Hayes, Dean Jackson, Dean Lorey, Deb Ingino, Debbie Phillips, Deborah Sweeney, Debra Sterling, Dee Ankary, Delatorro McNeal II, Derek Blair, Derek Coburn, Derek Miner, Derek Weber, Desiree Doubrox, Desiree Vargas Wrigley, Devin Thorpe, Dinesh Thiru, Dino Dogan, Dino Watt, Donald Miller, Donna Kozik, Dorie Clark, Douglas Goldstein, Dr. Bob Brooks, Dr. Isaac H. Jones, Drew Canole, Drew Meyers, Dusan Babich, Dustin Lee, Dustin Maher, Dwight Peters.

Elaine Heney, Elayna Fernandez, Elise Bialylew, Ellory Wells, Eric Bandholz, Eric Leuthardt, Eric Ries, Eric Schurenberg, Eric Siu, Eric Tivers, Erica Dhawan, Erick James, Erik Fisher, Erika Lyremark, Erin Giles, Esther Kiss, Evan Brand, Ezra Firestone.

Farnoosh Brock, Farnoosh Torabi, Fay Kitariev, Felicia Spahr, Felix Brandon Lloyd, Forbes Riley, Francis Pedraza, Frederique Campagne Irwin.

Gabriel Machuret, Garrett Gunderson, Garrett Moon, Gary Bizzo, Gary Leland, Gary Loper, Gary Swart, Gary Tessero, Geeta Nadkarni, Gene Hammett, Geordie Wardman, George Siosi Samuels, Gerald Rogers, Gideon Shalwick, Glen Allsopp, Grant Baldwin, Grant Cardone, Greg Bastin, Greg Hickman, Greg Hoffman, Greg Rollett, Greg Taylor, Gregory Ciotti, Gretchen Rubin, Griff Hanning, Guy Kawasaki.

Hal Elrod, Hans Finzel, Heather Carson, Herby Fabius, Hollis Carter, Honoree Corder, Howard Brown, Howard Marks, Hugh Culver.

Ian Cleary, Ian Schoen, Ivan Misner.

J.D. Roth, J.R. Johnson, Jack Canfield, Jackie Dinsmore, Jacob Kloberdanz, Jacob Sokol, Jadah Sellner, Jaime Tardy, Jake Ducey, Jake Larsen, Jake Weatherly, James Altucher, James Dalman, James Garvin, James Roche, James Scarmozzino, James Schramko, James Swanwick, James Woosley, Jan Stromsodd, Jan Winum, Jana Schuberth, Jared Easley, Jared Kleinert, Jason Falls, Jason Ferruggia, Jason Levesque, Jason Sadler, Jason Silverman, Jason Weisenthal, Jasper Ribbers, Jay Baer, Jay Miletsky, Jay Myers, Jay Samit, Jaydev Karande, Jayson Gaignard, Jeff Desjardins, Jeff Eckerle, Jeff Goins, Jeff Hays, Jeff Korhan, Jeff Moore, Jeff Rose, Jeff Schneider, Jeff Steinmann, Jeff Ullrich, Jeffrey Slater, Jen Groover, Jennifer Louden, Jennifer Paige, Jenny Blake, Jeremy Frandsen, Jeremy Reeves, Jerrod Sessler, Jesse Krieger, Jesse Mecham, Jessica Ekstrom, Jessica Kupferman, Jessica Turner, Jim Belosic, Jim Kukral, Jim Palmer, Jim Wang, Jimi Page, Jimmy Hayes, Joanna Penn, Jock Purtle, Joe Fairless, Joe Knight, Joe Mechlinski, Joe Palko, Joe Polish, Joe Pulizzi, Joel Comm, Joel Gascoigne, Joel Gross, Joel Widmer, John Ashworth, John Assaraf, John Caplan, John Corcoran, John Jantsch, John Jonas, John Lee Dumas, John Maddox, John McGinn, John McIntyre, John Ndege, Johnny B Truant, Jon Acuff, Jon Ferrara, Jon Gordon, Jon Morrow, Jon Nastor, Jon Stein, Jo-Na, Jonah Berger, Jonathan Fields, Jonathan Li, Jonathan Mead, Jonathan Merill, Jonathan Milligan, Jonathan Shank, Jordan Harbinger, Jordan Lloyd Bookey, Joseph Michael, Josh and Jill Stanton, Josh Escusa, Josh Ledgard, Josh London, Josh Mellicker, Josh Pigford, Josh Shipp, Joshua Becker, Joshua Parkinson, Judy Robinett, Julia Busha, Julia Tunstall, Julie Austin, Julie Morey, Jullien Gordon, Justin Baeder, Justin Brooke, Justin Gilchrist, Justin Harmon, Justin McCarthy,

Justin Mitchel, Justin Williams, JV Crum, Jyotsna
Ramachandran.

Kai Davis, Kane Minkus, Karen X. Cheng, Karim Abouelnaga,
Kate Marie Grinold Sigfusson, Kate Northrup, Katherine
Matsudaira, Katrina Starzhynskaya, Kaye Putnam, Keith
Kranc, Kelly Lundberg, Ken McArthur, Ken Sharrar, Kendall
Herbst, Kenneth Vogt, Kevin Clayson, Kevin Donahue, Kevin
Miller, Kevin Rogers, Kevin Thompson, Kim Nicol, Kimanzi
Constable, Kimberly Coleman, Kimberly Palmer, Korbett
Miller, Kris Gilbertson, Kristin Thompson, Kurt Elster, Kyle
Eschenroeder.

Lain Ehmann, LaJuan Stoxstill-Diggs, Landon Ray, Lara Ann
Riggio, Larry Benet, Larry Broughton, Laura Berg, Laura
Betterly, Laura Wagge, Laurel Staples, Lauren Solomon,
Laurie Brucker, Lee Frederiksen, Lee Hills, Lee LeFever, Leslie
Grossman, Leslie Samuel, Levi McPherson, Lewis Howes, Lian
Dolan, Lindsey Morando, Lisa B. Marshall, Lisa Parmley, Los
Silva, Ludwina Dautovic, Luke Iorio, Luke Liu, Luke Stokes.

Marc Angelo Coppola, Marcus Sheridan, Maria Ross, Marie
Forleo, Marilyn Tam, Marissa Levin, Marissa Sackler, Mark
Asquith, Mark Hoverson, Mark Jamnik, Mark Lack, Mark
LePage, Mark Schaefer, Mark Sisson, Marni Battista, Mary
Beth Storjohann, Mary Lou Kayser, Mary Marshall, Matt
Frazier, Matt Giovanisci, Matt Kepnes, Matt Kress, Matt
McWilliams, Matt Medeiros, Matt Paulson, Matt Theriault,
Matt Wheeler, Matt Wilson, Matthew Averkamp, Matthew
Jaskol, Max Altschuler, Max Teitelbaum, Mazarine Treyz,
Megan Gebhart, Melanie Benson, Melanie Duncan, Melinda
Fleming, Melvin Poh, Meredith Naughton, Meridith Elliott
Powell, Meron Bareket, Michael Crosson, Michael Epps Utley,
Michael Kawula, Michael Knouse, Michael Levin, Michael

Riscica, Michael Vigeant, Michael Wolf, Micheal Burt, Micheal O'Neal, Michel Issa, Mike Ambassador Bruny, Mike and Izabela Russell, Mike Blinder, Mike Cowles, Mike Del Ponte, Mike Dooley, Mike Hardenbrook, Mike Koenigs, Mike Krause, Mike Malloy, Mike Mandel, Mike Michalowicz, Mike Newton, Mike O'Hagan, Mike Thomas, Miki Agrawal, Mindy Gibbins-Klein, Minesh Bhindi, Misa Chien, Mish Slade, Mitch Gordon, Mitch Joel, Monica Hamilton, Montina Portis.

Nancy Duarte, Naomi Simson, Natalie MacNeil, Natasha Wescoat, Nate Bunger, Nate Dallas, Nathalie Lussier, Nathan Barry, Nathan Jurewicz, Nathan Latka, Nazrin Murphie, Neal Schaffer, Neen James, Neil Patel, Neil Willenson, Nella Chunky, Nellie Akalp, Nick Gray, Nick Loper, Nick Pavlidis, Nick Peall, Nick Reese, Nick Ruiz, Nick Unsworth, Nickhil Jakatdar, Nicole Jolie, Nicole Lapin, Nikhil Arora, Noah St. John, Norm Bour.

Ophelie Lechat, Oren Klaff, Owen McGab Enaohwo.

Pace Smith, Pam Hendrickson, Pamela O'Hara, Pamela Slim, Pat Flynn, Pat Romain, Patrick Galvin, Patrick Gentempo, Patrick Lehoux, Patrick Llewellyn, Patrick M. Powers, Patrick Pettitt, Patrick Schwerdtfeger, Paul Colligan, Paul Copcutt, Paul Jarrett, Paul Kushnir, Peep Laja, Pejman Ghadimi, Penny Sansevieri, Perry Marshall, Peter Radcliffe, Peter Reinhardt, Peter Shallard, Peter Shankman, Phil Masiello, Phil Rogers, Philip Taylor, Phyllis Khare, PJ Jonas, Priscilla Stephan.

Quinn & Jonathon, Quy Vo.

Rabet Brown, Racheal Cook, Rachel Cruze, Rachel Hanfling, Rachel Martin, Rakesh Soni, Ralph Quintero, Ram Ramkumar, Raoul Anderson, Ray Gillenwater, Ray Higdon,

Rebecca Livermore, Reed ShaffnerRegina Busse, Renee Airya,
Renee Warren, Rhonda Cort, Ric Dragon, Rich Horwath,
Richard Botto, Richard Rierson, Richelle Shaw, Richie Norton,
Rick Day, Rick Mulready, Rick Sapio, Rob Dix, Rob Bellenfant,
Rob Bence, Rob Cubbon, Rob Montana, Rob Rawson, Robbie
Friedman, Robert Coorey, Robert Farrington, Robert Graham,
Robert Greene, Robert Hirsch, Robert Richman, Robert
Wasser, Roberto Candelaria, Robin Hallett, Rod Drury, Roger
Lee, Rohit Bhargava, Rory Vaden, Rosh Khan, Russell
Brunson, Ryan Blair, Ryan Cote, Ryan Daniel Moran, Ryan
Delk, Ryan Jenkins, Ryan Kekos, Ryan Lee, Ryan Levesque,
Ryan MicKinney, Ryan Waier, Ryan Westwood.

Sally Hogshead, Sam Horn, Samantha Bell, Samantha Quist,
Sandi Lin, Sandra Singh, Sandy Connery, Sara Davidson,
Sarah Robinson, Saul Of-Hearts, Savitha Rao, Scott Britton,
Scott Cramton, Scott Dinsmore, Scott Jordan, Scott
Martineau, Scott McKain, Scott Oldford, Scott Skinger, Scott
Smith, Sean Ellis, Sean Malarkey, Sean Marshall, Sean Ogle,
Sean Stephenson, Selena Soo, Seth Godin, Seth Goldstein,
Shane & Jocelyn Sams, Shane Stott, Shannon Kinney, Shawn
Collins, Shawn Stevenson, Sheila Viers, Sherisse Hawkins,
Shlomy Kattan, Simon Bailey, Simon Czaplinski, Skinner
Layne, Sohail Khan, Sol Orwell, Sophia Bera, Spencer Haws,
Srinivas Rao, Stella Fayman, Steph Halligan, Stephan Aarstol,
Stephanie Burns, Stephanie O'Brien, Stephanie Wetzel,
Stephen Key, Stephen Woessner, Steve Cherubino, Steve Cook,
Steve Daar, Steve Greenbaum, Steve Gumm, Steve Nixon,
Steve Olsher, Steve Richardson, Steve Scott, Steven Memel,
Stu McLaren, Stuart Crane, Stuart Knight, Sunil Rajaraman,
Susan RoAne, Susan Weinschenk, Syed Balkhi.

Tammy Levent, Tara Mohr, Terry Lin, Tess Strand, Thom
Hunt, Thom Singer, Thomas Shajan, Tiffany Peterson, Tim

Ferriss, Tim Grahl, Tim Johnson, Tim Nybo, Tim Roberts, Timo Kiander, Tina Forsyth, Toby Jenkins, Todd Garland, Todd Henry, Tom Corley, Tom Kuhn, Tom Morkes, Tom Schwab, Tom Ziglar, Tommie Powers, Tommy Walker, Tony Stubblebine, Tracy Matthews, Tracy Osborn, Travis Ketchum, Travis Thorpe, Trent Dyrsmid, Trevor Blake, Trevor Page, Tricia Meyer, Troy Broussard, Troy Dean, Tyler Simpson.

Uddy Carmi.

Valerie Young, Vanae, Vanessa Maddox, Vanessa Van Edwards, Vasavi Kumar, VaShaun Jones, Vernon Foster II, Vince Reed, Vinnie Tortorich, Viveka von Rosen.

Warren Bobrow, Wes Eisenhauer, Wes Shaeffer, Will Mitchell, Will Swayne, Willem Sodderland, William Shaker, Woody Woodward.

Yamile Yemoonyah, Yanik Silver, Yaslynn Mack, Yasmine Arrington, Yifat Cohen, Yuri Elkhaim.

Zac Johnson, Zack O'Malley Greenburg, Zechariah Newman, Zvi Band.

About the Author

Nick Loper is an online entrepreneur and lifelong student in the game of business. He lives in Northern California with his wife Bryn and a lovable giant Shih-Tzu called Mochi. On a typical day you can find him writing, working on his latest business idea, rooting for the Huskies, or skiing the Sierra pow.

Nick built his first website in 2003, and was instantly hooked. Since then he's run a number of small online businesses and consulted for dozens more.

Always on the lookout for ways to work smarter and get more done, this list of resources was a natural project and a lot of fun to compile.

As you can probably tell from the book, he gets really excited about this stuff and wants to help other entrepreneurs find success online.

Want to know more? Drop by and check out his blog, SideHustleNation.com, a growing resource and community for aspiring and part-time entrepreneurs.

Or feel free to say hi on Twitter (@nloper).

Do you have an online resource you'd like to share? Get in touch and you might just be featured in the next edition of this book!

Thank You!

I'd like to say a quick "thank you" for purchasing this book.

Obviously there are thousands of books out there, but you took a chance and chose this one.

Hopefully it got the gears turning and you learned of some new tools and resources to help you in your business.

As a special bonus gift, be sure to grab a free copy of *53 Takeaways from the World's Best Business Books*:

http://www.sidehustlenation.com/FREE

If you have any questions or feedback, please let me know (nick@sidehustlenation.com). Your comments are really valuable because they will guide future editions of this book and I'm always striving to improve my writing.

And if you liked what you read, I need your help!

Please take a minute to leave a quick review on Amazon.

Thanks so much!

Also by Nick

Nick is also the author of:

The Side Hustle Path: 10 Proven Ways to Make Money Outside of Your Day Job

The Side Hustle Path Volume 2: 10 Proven Ways to Make Money Outside of Your Day Job

The Small Business Website Checklist: A 51-Point Guide to Build Your Online Presence The Smart Way

Treadmill Desk Revolution: The Easy Way to Lose Up to 50 Pounds in a Year – Without Dieting

Virtual Assistant Assistant: The Ultimate Guide to Finding, Hiring, and Working with Virtual Assistants

40562764R00083

Made in the USA
Middletown, DE
16 February 2017